Making Sentences

Lisa Peterson

www.peterson-jensica.com

L.P.

This is a copyright protected publication. The book is designed to be a teacher resource. If you are interested in other publications or presentations please contact me.

Copying for <u>student use only</u> is permitted on the black line master pages (70-112)

No other written or illustrated part of this book may be copied without express permission of the author. Unauthorized copying will not be tolerated.

Order this book online at www.trafford.com/06-3299
or email orders@trafford.com

Most Trafford titles are also available at major online book retailers.

Note for Librarians: A cataloguing record for this book is available from Library and Archives Canada at www.collectionscanada.ca/amicus/index-e.html

Printed in Victoria, BC, Canada.

ISBN: 978-1-4251-1549-4

We at Trafford believe that it is the responsibility of us all, as both individuals and corporations, to make choices that are environmentally and socially sound. You, in turn, are supporting this responsible conduct each time you purchase a Trafford book, or make use of our publishing services. To find out how you are helping, please visit www.trafford.com/responsiblepublishing.html

Our mission is to efficiently provide the world's finest, most comprehensive book publishing service, enabling every author to experience success. To find out how to publish your book, your way, and have it available worldwide, visit us online at www.trafford.com/10510

Trafford PUBLISHING™ www.trafford.com

North America & international
toll-free: 1 888 232 4444 (USA & Canada)
phone: 250 383 6864 ♦ fax: 250 383 6804 ♦ email: info@trafford.com

The United Kingdom & Europe
phone: +44 (0)1865 722 113 ♦ local rate: 0845 230 9601
facsimile: +44 (0)1865 722 868 ♦ email: info.uk@trafford.com

10 9 8 7 6 5 4 3 2

Table of Contents

Being a teacher is like a bird building a nest, we take a twig from here or there, a thread, a piece of wool and create a 'home' of our own. ***L. Peterson***

The material I present in Making Sentences is not brand new but based on the learning I have undergone since I began teaching in 1986. I became a teacher because of my first grade teacher Mrs. Beth Lillieur. She had a way of making learning meaningful and personal to each student. She used frame sentences to create a feeling of success, and as I began my career I learned about the frame sentences used by the McCracken's. I have expanded upon such frame sentences and organized a sequenced lesson format, games and activities for introducing sight words, concept words and sentence structure.

These activities and approaches can be extended to older or more advanced students by focusing on vocabulary from content areas as well as literature selections. Sentence starters can be extended to phrase strips to encourage more sophisticated and grammatically correct compositions.

As teachers, we are constantly learning ourselves, seeing or hearing an idea, expanding and altering ideas to make them our own and to match them to our students needs. As you read and use Making Sentences you may see familiar ideas, I have endeavored to include references that have inspired me over the years, I apologize if I have missed any.

Thank you to Jennifer Peterson for designing the cover and Web site for Making Sentences. My appreciation to the following colleagues who provided proofreading, editing and suggestions; Tazmin Manji, Lynda Petersen, Terrie Sisk, Lynn Williams, Louise Graham and Kimberly Franklin. I am forever thankful to my Lord for guidance.

www.peterson-jensica.com

Welcome to Making Sentences

Making Sentences is a method of teaching reading and writing for beginning students and extending and building upon skills for older or more capable students. This method offers step-by-step word introduction and assists the teacher in tailoring the learning to fit each child. The words chosen come from student experiences, their prior knowledge and include both sight and phonetic words to create functional reading and writing which relates to each child's experiences. This is a great resource for teachers or home school parents.

Fountas and Pinnell in 'Word Matters' refer to what makes an effective word-learning program. They have identified the following points as good teaching practices for effective language programs:

- Engaging learners in conversations about words in various chart and word displays.
- Working together to create charts and displays of work that develop over time.
- Looking at principles rather than memorizing letters and word.
- Building upon student knowledge base and connecting to new learning.
- Having learning about letters and words be interesting and exciting.
- Working at the students level. (Fountas/Pinnell 1998)

Making Sentences uses high frequency, sight and phonetic Word Cards, Sentence Starters, Word Wall Displays, Word Searches, Cloze, games and various writing activities to teach reading and sentence formation. All of these activities build and reinforce the vocabulary being introduced. These activities also provide opportunities for the teacher to develop sight word and phonemic approaches to reading. Students are able to develop decoding and sight word skills as well as increasing their fluency. As word introduction progresses, plurals and other word endings and tenses will be added to the students writing. Personal interest words are also introduced, as each student requires. The sentence writing and copying allows the teacher to reinforce the use of capitalization and punctuation in sentences at an early stage. The sentences and subsequent stories increase in complexity according to the increasing skills of the students. Students are engaged and interested in reading and writing about their own thoughts and experiences. Phrase strips are an extension for older students, teaching more sophisticated writing, note gathering and organizing. Selecting main ideas, sequencing and working with vocabulary and concepts extend students skills.

The Making Sentences program provides opportunities for students to learn, practice and master reading and writing skills. They use their prior knowledge, and familiarity with the theme words to build strong foundational reading and writing abilities. Examples of skills gained are:

Reading short illustrated selections on their own
Demonstrating confidence
Using phonics
Using illustrations to assist in comprehension
Using prior knowledge in reading
Using print conventions such as question marks
Recognizing many common sight words
Using word families to read new words

Young students' writing will display:

Personal experiences in writing
Sentences that relate to each other
Sentences that display some detail
Repetitive sentences and patterns
Use of pronouns
Use of tense
Invented spelling
Conventional spelling of familiar words
Phonetic spelling for unfamiliar words
Use of some punctuation
Writing with some independence
Plural matching with linking verbs
Adjectives and adverbs

Older students' will also display:

Cohesive paragraph construction
Comprehension and inferring skills
Grammatically correct sentence structure
Note taking skills
Organization skills in writing
Oral language and listening skills
Proof reading and editing skills
Word substitution awareness

Connections

Making connections is the basis to making meaningful and memorable learning.

Current research on Brain development and memory retention indicates that students need to work within clear expectations, to experience a feeling of empowerment and to feel free to take risks. Research and assessments of and for learning clearly point to the vital importance of prompt and descriptive feedback. (Wolfe)(Lombardi)

The social nature and hands on structure of Making Sentences allows the teacher to move with ease from one student to another observing word recognition, sentence formation and sophistication. The teacher is able to clearly see students demonstrating personal strengths and learning needs. Basing learning on prior knowledge, making connections from those experiences to new learning experiences and social interactions is an express route to making learning meaningful and memorable.

The social and interactive elements of Making Sentences create opportunities for multiple connections such as:

- student to student connections in conversation, experiences and learning.
- Student to teacher connections in evaluating learning and creating learning relationships.
- Student to reading and writing connections are prevalent because the reading is related to their own experiences.

The more connections that students can make to learning, the more memory retention they will have. Picture, if you will, a map to your favourite place. Picture that place infiltrated with secret pathways that you can use to go there, and, because you know so many ways to get there you can do so with speed and ease and confidence. Students who make multiple connections to learning through linking prior experiences, interactive learning experiences, social and cooperative learning, oral language, and prompt feedback create those quick and easy ways to access their learning (Wolfe). If we can facilitate the building of connections to map out effective learning we should, and if we can do that in a fun and engaging way – lets do it.

Making Sentences and Guided Reading

Making Sentences is a valuable part to any Guided Reading program and is an effective way to begin your reading lessons each day. The teacher can address many essential strategies such as sounding out, skipping, rereading, reading on, and meaningful substitution.

Making Sentences is a valuable tool with which to build and assess the students' understanding and use of visual [graphophonic] cues as well as context and picture cues. The guided practice that the teacher can provide strategically builds upon syntax [grammar] cues.

Repetition of the vocabulary in sentences is an advantage because it allows continued exposure and practice. This repetition also allows the student to advance from word by word reading towards fluency. You will notice in the mini book section that many of the sentences are arranged in phrases to support fluency in reading. Mini books can be used in class as a part of your reading center or personal reading time and can be used as part of your home reading program.

Guided Reading Literacy Center Connection

Each of the following activities and games can be set out as literacy centers around your classroom.

Sentence Flip Strips p.42
Personal Books p.46
Write and Read Homework Books p.47
Diagrams and Cartoons p. 48
Sentence Matching p.58
Sentence Scramble p.59
Dive In p.60
Rhyme It p.62
Drama and Charades p. 64
Sentence Cubes p. 64
Instead of Said p. 65
Mini Books p.44
Read and Riddle p. 57
Contractions p.61
Compound Words p.61
Journal p.51
Eloquent Expressions p.50
Poem Detectives p. 55

Sentence Flip Strip materials can be pre-made and available in a basket, complete with pencils, erasers and crayons. The teacher may have a sample made up to help children identify words by pictures clues to further enhance their independence. Students will complete this activity independently while working in a small group.

Mini Books can be copied, folded and stapled by a parent helper and set out in a basket just as the Sentence Flip Strips. Again, a sample book or labelled pictures will help with independence and success. Students will complete this activity independently while working in a small group.

Sentence Matching and Sentence Scrambles can be set up as separate centers. Each requires partner work.

Dive In is a small group center activity with participants cooperating to complete the game.

Write and Read homework books become a part of a quiet reading center. They may be read individually or shared.

Blank 'Personal Books' can be pre-made and available in a basket, with pencils, erasers, crayons and glue and a selection of blank sentence strips. In addition, the teacher may choose to have available a basket of corresponding pictures from stamps, cards, magazines etc. to be cut out and glued in.

Invented Spelling

'Personal books' have a second important job in this program. Although Making Sentences provides words to assist students in their writing, invented spelling is a valuable component. When students are writing and they want a word that they currently do not have, they need to be encouraged to try to spell their own words. Invented spelling builds student confidence in personal abilities and growth (Goodman).

Invented spelling also provides the teacher with clues as to each child's skill level as well as topics for future teaching topics. When a student uses an invented spelling word in his or her own writing, I recommend leaving it as is or writing the conventional form underneath. If the student wants that new word on a card for future use, the teacher will put it on a word card as a personal or special word. Students are also encouraged to print invented spelling words on blank word cards. Allowing them to do this provides students with the self-confidence needed to take risks. Accepting their invented spelling tells the student that you value their efforts and ideas.

Invented spelling is a celebration; the student is displaying independence and trust in his or her own skills. Making Sentences word card provides a resource for student writing. It provides a structure from which to develop skills, but it is also essential that students feel encouraged to use invented spelling within Making Sentences.

Ready Get Set –Go

I invite you to follow this format for implementation of each sentence starter or group of new words. Making Sentences integrates learning activities and games to create an engaging learning environment.

- First you may introduce word cards for the sentence starter by playing the **Show Me Tell Me** game. p.56
- **Introduce a sentence starter** and have children match your example, play rhyming games or I'm thinking of a word that starts with a ___ , any activity that helps the students focus on the look and sounds of the selected word cards. *The suggested sentence starter sequence follows this section.*
- Display your sentence starter and have students match it. Then practice reading it together. Have students point to the words as you read them.
- Use the **Sentence Flip Strips** activity found on page 42 to practice both writing and reading. As children use the sentence starter on the strip they become comfortable with the reading pattern. The flips allow them to illustrate and make memory connections to the additional words you have selected for the sentences. As children become more and more capable you may individualize this accordingly. When the labour of writing decreases the teacher may choose to move from flip strips to personal books detailed on page 46.
- **Mini books** can be created to reflect the growing vocabulary. Using the same words and sentences you can create these mini books, which the students illustrate and read (p. 44 and 91).

I recommend that this format be followed with the introduction of each new sentence starter. The games set out in this program can be used as part of each lesson or as a literacy center.

Sentence Starters – step by step introduction

The 'How to do it' section

The following are the first three sentence starters with which to start (McCracken). The words to put into the sentences are suggestions to which the teacher can add or delete as words are matched to the needs of the children. I have chosen words suitable for a playground or park theme so children can easily relate and think of their own experiences. Establishing a link to background knowledge is valuable in all aspects of reading and writing development.

- I can
- I see
- I like

1- I can – sentence starter

Beginning with the 'I can' sentence starter the teacher is able to focus on a few select words and immediately create a sense of success for the students. Using words that have been generated by students, the teacher can help the student create these sentences. Run, play, swing, slide, hide, ride, skate are examples of some student words.

I can run.	I can swing.
I can play.	I can ride.
I can swing.	I can hide.

Hint – *Keep a plentiful stack of blank coloured word cards in a small gift size box so students may access it to print new personal words and blank white cards to replace lost group word cards. When a student loses a word card it is his/her job to get a blank card and copy the missing word from a buddy. I stress the importance of students solving their own problems. I believe they are capable and they always prove me right.*

2- I see – sentence starter

As the children become comfortable with variations on the **'I can…'** starter the teacher may move on to the **'I see…'** starter. This sentence starter allows the teacher the opportunity to teach **'a'** and **'plurals'**. Making sentences with the cards, allows the teacher the opportunity to add on **'s'** cards to create plurals.

[a] boy, girl, cat, dog, park, house, school, swings, slides, bike, tree, motorcycle (motorcycle is an example of a word a child may want, it is up to the teacher to use it as a class word or as a personal word for that child)

Endings such as s ,es, ed, ing, er, est may be added by copying 'word ending cards' which can be placed under the existing word cards to create the new form.

I see **a** boy.	I see **a** girl.	I see **a** cat.
I see **a** dog.	I see **a** park.	I see **a** bike.
I see swing**s**.	I see slide**s**.	I see tree**s**.

These sentences may seem simple to you, but to the child this offers success and ownership of learning through the words they select to accompany the sentence starters.

Each step of the way the teacher will want to add and exchange words in the sentence starters. Every time new words are added the child and teacher should play the Show Me Tell Me game to practice and increase recall of the working vocabulary words.

Sentence Extensions

The next step is to challenge the child to create a variety of sentences such as:

I can see a boy.
I see a park.
I can play.
A girl can play.
A boy can hide.
I can ride a bike.

I can see trees.
See the dogs play.
I see a big orange cat.
A big girl can ride.
I can ride a little bike.
See the big dog run.

Introducing 'big' and 'little' allows for further extensions of sentences. Adding adjectives such as big and little and colour words also provides a platform for using the classroom chart or word wall in all kinds of classroom writing. (Cunningham 1995)

After allowing your students to work with these extensions you will introduce the words **'the'** and **'and'**. These two words will allow the children to build longer sentences such as:

I can see a boy **and** girl.
I can see **the** big park.
The girl can run **and** hide.
The boy can play **and** slide.
I can play.
I can run.
I see a little cat run.
The cat hides.
I can see a dog run.
The dog runs **and the** cat runs.

*Teaching them at this level to limit the use of **'and'** in sentence writing will be of great value as they become more prolific.*

*Any word such as **'The'**, which can be used either to begin a sentence or within a sentence can be double sided so one side displays capitalization. **See** and **Can** may also be capitalized for beginning sentences.*

You may also have them use names of their friends or family members at this stage. This allows for the sentences to become more personal and interesting to the students.

I can see Tanner and Lauren.
Dale can see the park.
Jessica can run and hide.
Jennifer can play and slide.
Graham can play.
Andrea can run.

3- I like sentence starter

This sentence starter can use many of the same word cards and provides an opportunity to personalize the child's sentences even more. This sentence starter is the perfect place to introduce the use of **'to'** and **'the'** into sentences.

As a sentence starter, 'I like' allows students to bring some personal words into Making Sentences. In addition to the 'park' theme words (cats, dogs, pets, bikes, soccer, playing, basketball, drawing) students may add personal word choices.

Vocabulary reflecting personal interests is often more difficult than adults would choose for children, but the opportunity for children to have this involvement in their reading and writing and learning at this early stage of development is vital in establishing a sense of interest and ownership. Children may choose to write, **" I like motorcycles"** or **" I like spaghetti"** or **" I like Dinopolous"** – the newest cartoon hero. The chosen words may appear difficult but because they come from personal interest and are supported with child created illustrations they children recall them with surprisingly little hesitation.

Now the teacher can call upon 3 sentence starters and will provide the assistance needed so that the students can create more and more sentences. Encourage them to combine words to create more complex sentences such as:

I can see a big boy and a girl.
I see a dog and a cat.
I like pets.
I like the park.
Andrea can slide and play.
I like to run and run.
Jess can swing.
I like to hide.

I see a big motorcycle.
I like motorcycles.
Jen can ride to the park.
Kirby can run and play.
I like Dinopolous.
Dinopolous can hide.
Dinopolous can play and run.
*** Dinopolous can be invisible.**

Often children will be excited about a personal word or character and will need support from the teacher to get new words to support what they want to write with the cards. It is important that if a child wants to express something that we provide the tools to do so. Special words such as **'Dinopolous can be invisible'** can be written on a different colour of card to make using them easier.

75 Sentences

Having only introduced **3** sentence starters and **25** words cards from the sample list, children could make all of the following 75 sentences and more.
I, can, see, like, run, play, swing, slide, hide, ride, a, boy, girl, cat, dog, park, bike, pets, to, the, and, tree, big, little, motorcycle.

I can see.
I can run.
I can see a girl.
I like parks.
I see a big bike.
I like pet**s**.
I like bike**s**.

I can ride.
I see pets.
I see a little cat.
I can swing.
I see a ride.
I like to play.
I like to hide.

I see a swing.
I see a big slide.
I can see a girl.
I see a dog.
I see a park.
I like to slide.
I like to bike.

I can see boy**s**.
I can play.
I see a pet.
I can hide.
I like to run.
I like to play.
I like to ride.

I like to swing.
I can run and play.
I can swing and play.
I can run and hide.
I can ride a little motorcycle.
I can see a dog and a cat.
The boy can ride the motorcycle.
I can ride and ride.
The boy can see the bike.
I like motorcycle**s**.
I like swing**s** and slide**s**.
I like to see cat**s** play.
I like to see a boy play.
I like to see a dog slide.
I like to pet the little dog.
I like girl**s** and boy**s**.
A dog like**s** to run.
The cat like**s** to run and hide.
I like to ride the bike to the park.
I like to see the dog and cat run.
See the cat and dog run.
Can the cat hide?
Can the dog run to the cat?

I see a motorcycle.
I can see a boy and a girl.
I can see a dog park.
I can see a cat and a dog run.
The dog and cat can run to the park.
The boy and girl can run to the park.
A girl can ride a motorcycle.
I can ride a motorcycle to the park.
The girl can see the bike.
I can ride the bike.
I like cats and dog**s**.
I like to see dog**s** play.
I like to see a girl play.
I like to see the cat hide.
I like to pet the cat.
I like to run and hide.
I can see boy**s** and girl**s**.
I can play in the trees.
I like to hide in the tree.
I see the cat run to the tree.
See, I can ride and ride.
See the big boy ride the big bike.
Can you play?

I like to see the dog run and the cat hide.
The girl can ride the big motorcycle to the park.
A boy can ride a motorcycle to the park.

Having completed the first three sentence starters you and your students are well on the way to successful reading and writing.

4- **I went** and **I saw sentence starters** – Introducing Tense

Teaching the use of tense is accomplished through introducing the word **'saw'** and **'went'** which allows the children to create may of the same sentences in the past tense rather than the present. This is where the written language they are creating with the sentence cards begins to resemble ' real language'. Adding these sentence starters creates even more sentences to be read and written.

I went to the park and saw a dog and cat.

I saw a boy run to the bike and ride to the park.

The little cat went to hide.

Jen saw Kirby run and hide.

Remember that word endings such as **s, es, ed, ing, er, est** *can be introduced as needed. Suffixes may be printed onto word cards and placed on a word to create the change in tense. For words that require an* **'ied'** *change in ending the card is placed over the letter receiving the change.*

Children with English as their first language will often automatically insert these word endings when reading sentences (even if the ending is not physically there) Most of these children naturally 'hear' these endings.

Children who have ESL (English as a Second Language) will benefit from the Making Sentences structure as the teacher focuses on their specific learning needs.

5- **I am – sentence starter** - Introducing **'ing'** endings

The children are now able to write a significant amount of basic sentences. Now you can begin using 'ing' words with the sentence starter **'I am'.** Using **'I am'** the teacher may revisit many of the words previously used but by adding **'ing'** onto the ending. For example the early sentences like
I can run or **I can play** become **I am running** or I **am playing**.

I am running.

I am playing.

I am riding.

As a further extension the teacher may also introduce the word cards 'going' and 'to

I am going to the park.

I am going to play soccer.

I am going to run and hide.

6- I was – sentence starters

Continuing with the 'ing' words used in the 'I am' sentence starter the teacher can once again reinforce the concept of tense. Relying on previous words the children can create even more sentences.

I was playing.

I was riding the bike.

I was running.

As a further extension the teacher may also introduce **'going'** to the sentence starter.

I was going to play soccer.

I was going to the park.

I was going to pet the dog.

Words such as ***'in'*** *or* ***'on'*** *may be taught as needed.*

I was playing on the slide.

I was playing in the park.

I was hiding in the trees.

By this time the students have had success creating simple sentences. They are reading and using cards to make sentences. It is important to add adjectives and adverbs as well as allowing students to add personal words to their selections. Adding the adverb 'fast' can bring more to their sentences.

I was riding fast.

The big dog was running fast.

The motorcycle was going fast.

7- Introducing Singular Pronouns as sentence starters

She can…	He can…	She likes…	He likes…
She saw...	He saw…	She went…	He went…

Incorporating **she** and **he** is a natural addition at this time in the Making Sentences program. We build upon the students' repertoire of sentences by adding **he** and **she** and **him** and **her** into the sentences with which they are already comfortable. A sentence such as **I like motorcycles** becomes **She likes motorcycles.**

This also provides the opportunity for the teacher to continue plural formation with the addition of the 's' to some words.

She saw Jess run and hide.

I saw her run and hide.

He saw her run and hide.

8- Introducing plural pronouns as sentence starters

Revisiting previously learned sentences the teacher may introduce the pronouns **they** and **we.**

We can ride.

We can run and play.

They like going to the park.

Introducing the word card **'at'** after the pronouns allows the students to have practice with all the pronouns while learning how to use 'at'.

They like to play at the park.

We went riding at the park.

She is at the slide.

9- We were / They were – as sentence starters

This sentence starter continues the reinforcement the concept of tense and matching of pronouns to linking verbs. Relying on previous words the children can create even more sentences.

We were playing.

They are riding bikes.

We were running.

Review spent at this time to practice matching of tense and plural or singular linking verbs is important at this time.

I was riding.	They were riding.
He was playing.	We were playing.
She is running.	They are running.
I am sliding.	We are sliding.

While taking this time to practice tenses it convenient to work with words such as has – has and run – ran.

Where Am I ?– take a look at the progress

The Teacher may notice students rely less and less on moving the word cards to make sentences. As their skills grow they will be able to write sentences with less word card support. They can be encouraged to use the word cards as needed in their personal writing.

Continue to use the word card sentence-making format for new sentence starters and with class jobs and homework. The continued structure provides a familiar work situation and increased independence. As they students become more and more independent with Making Sentences the teacher is able to focus less on management and more on the details of student learning.

10- **Look at …- sentence starters**

After spending time introducing 'at' with the pronouns the teacher will be able to move through this sentence starter with ease. **Look at…** provides a motivating sentence starter for the students to make silly sentences in addition to the basic theme word sentences. Individualized words will enter the scene with this starter.

Look at the purple gorilla.

Look at the big green bug.

Look at Dinopolous.

The word cards **'me'** and **'them'** may be brought in at this time for simple sentences such as;

Look at me.

Look I can run.

Look at them play soccer.

The word card **'for'** may also be used at this time to create sentences such as:

Look for the cat.

Look for me.

Look for Graham.

Remember any word that can also start a sentence needs to be a double-sided card or use two cards with a capital and lower case version.

I introduce the word **'home'** at this time so the students can create more variety in their sentences. The use of 'home' encourages students to ask for more personal words and consequently increases their vocabulary. I use 'home' because it links easily to going to the park.

11- Linking verbs is and are into sentence starters

This is a time to revisit the **'ing'** ending introduced with sentence starter **#5 I am.** Use these endings with **is** and **are**.

She is running.	She is riding a bike.
He is swinging.	He is hiding the bike.
We are playing.	We are going to home.

This allows for the plural pronouns to be matched correctly to the linking verbs. *This is a concept that is worth spending additional time to master.*

12- **There and Here as sentence starters**

Continuing to use all the prior words new sentences can be made using **There** and **Here**.

There are the cats.	Here are the dogs.
There is the park.	Here are the swings.
There is the slide.	Here is her home.

The word cards **'come'** and **'came'** can be easily introduced with the **'There'** and **'Here'** sentence starters.

Here come the girls.

They came to the park.

We came to play.

13- **Introducing future tense sentence starters**

Combining the previously learned pronouns with the word **'will'** allows the teacher to introduce future tense as well as once again create more sentences.

I will… She will… He will… They will…. We will…

I will come to the park to play.

She will go to play.

We will ride the bikes home.

14- **Will you … is the follow-up sentence starter**

This continues to build upon future tense while introducing the new word 'you'.

The word card **'with'** can be integrated into the sentences as this point.

Will you play with her?	Will you come to the park?
I will play with her.	Will I play with you?
Will she play with me?	Can I play with you?

Will you…sets up questions and allows new punctuation to be officially introduced.

Children have already experimented with using 'Can' to begin a sentence therefore already learning about asking a question. Using 'will you' allows the teacher to focus on questioning.

15- **I learned… - sentence starters**

This is a very powerful sentence starter because it allows children to identify all the things that they have accomplished. Students will want to use personal words in this activity. With this sentence starter the teacher may choose to make a memory book in addition to the other activities and keep it as a portfolio element. At this point in the Making Sentences program the students may be ready for even more individualized words. After exploring **I learned…** the other pronouns may be applied to extend the writing and reading.

I learned to ride.

She learned to play the drums. (use of personal word choices)

They learned to play the game. (use of personal word choices)

Using this starter the teacher can lead the students in making a Memory Book, simply copy the cover p.107 and use it with the personal book format. The ' I learned ' sentence starter can be a valuable tool is assessing student growth and student's awareness of their own learning journey.

16- **I tried…- sentence starters**

Similarly to the **'I learned…'** starter, **I tried** is a very positive self-evaluating topic. It is important for students to believe that their efforts are valuable. Working with **I learned**… first, gives them a feeling of accomplishment. Following that with **I tried**… gives the teacher a reference point with which to help the student move on to even more learning.

I tried to play with him.

She tried to ride the big bike to the park.

They tried to run home fast.

17- **I have…** and **I did… - sentence starters**

Pronouns are reviewed easily with this sentence starter. New vocabulary individually matched to the students may also be introduced at this point.

I have played with Jen.

I did have fun.

I have learned to ride.

Again touching on the usage of tenses the teacher can introduce the word 'had' and practice these sentences.

I had fun.

They had the bikes.

We had a little swing.

18- **I want – sentence starters**

Students often have fun with this sentence starter. Being that they have experience making sentences and they now have many sight words and sounding out skills, students are ready to explore personal words. At this point in making sentences the students will be asking how to spell words that they want to use. They will be able to leave the theme words you have introduced.

I want to be a chiropractor.

I want a kitten.

I want to go to Long Beach.

19- **I said-sentence starters –Introducing Quotations**

This is a very important sentence starter because it provides the opportunity to teach about quotations and punctuation. Using the students' knowledge of names, pronouns, tenses, and mastered vocabulary they can begin making sentences such as:

Graham said, "I can ride a bike to the park."

I said, "I learned to ride a bike."

She said, "I want to learn to ride a bike"

Using coloured strips for the quotation portion of a sentence and a separate colour strip for the speaker clearly shows the students that identification of the speaker is an essential element.

Hand out shorter ' yellow ' strips about 8 cm. long for the students to identify the speaker. Hand out 'blue' strips about 13 cm. long for the students to write what the speaker is saying. Matching these two strips together and then copying them into a personal book provides the reminder they often need to include the speaker identification.

We have to remember that the student writer knows who the speaker is in their story; they just don't understand that the reader doesn't get it.

Soon students will be reading and writing sentences that demonstrate punctuation and speaker identification. So often the writing of young students does not identify speakers and the flow of the story can be difficult to follow. Introducing this as a part of making sentences provides the opportunity to have children understand and become in the 'habit' of using speaker identification.

20- **Focusing on questioning – sentence starters**

Sentence starter 14 **Will you…** was the first official introduction of questioning. Students will now be ready to create a variety of questions using new word cards. The teacher can guide the students into creating questions around 'Will Could Would'

Will you play?

Could I come to the park?

Would Jennifer like to play?

The word cards **'ask'** and **'asked** will allow the teacher to continue the use of speaker identification and quotation marks that had been introduced in the previous sentence starter. Quotation colour strips from #19 may continue to be used with this questioning focus. The separate strip and colours makes the matching of speaker to quotation so much easier for the students.

"Will you play with me?" asked Jess.

"Could I go to the park?" asked Jennifer.

"Would you ask Graham to play soccer?" asked Talia.

As part of their homework, students may begin taking home colour strips to use in addition to the word cards.

Relating Show and Tell questioning to Making Sentences questioning can create links for children between their experiences and the introduction of new concepts. Show and Tell provides opportunities for interactions between students. Questions brought forward in this venue can be added to your word cards to extend variety and vocabulary.

Extending for Older Students

As you can tell, Making Sentences is not just for beginning readers and writers but can provide the scaffolding needed for your older students. Instead of using solely word cards the teacher may introduce phrase strips. The games can be adapted and extended to match developed skill levels. Content areas can be the focus of vocabulary selection for Making Sentences. The sentences may then be arranged and grouped to create cohesive paragraphs.

What's My Word

Instead of playing 'Dive In', older students can play 'What's My Word'. This is very effective for content areas. As an example, in grade 3 Plant Science, word cards from their science allow the students to demonstrate their knowledge. Playing " What's My Word" requires students to provide hints, descriptions or definitions to a partner therefore solidifying their understanding of the vocabulary and providing the necessary rehearsals to set to memory.

Word cards may also be used to create a guideline for summarizing knowledge. The teacher may select vocabulary from a content area or piece of literature. Then the students use those word cards to create a summarizing paragraph. The student formulates a sentence for each word and records the sentences on strips. The strips can then be sequenced to create the best paragraph possible. Additional descriptive words may be added with ease. Writing conventions can be proofread and edited with partners before the work in put to paper. This results in quality writing without going through a process of draft to good copy printing. By providing the students with the selected vocabulary the paragraph will result in 'on topic' sentences.

After the students experience success with creating paragraphs from teacher selected word cards, the students may work in partners to select the 'main topic' words from a text selection. The partner component requires them to discuss and agree on the most important concepts. This is a particularly valuable strategy for the students to develop the necessary skills for selecting important elements and composing summaries or research essays.

Another approach to developing summarizing skills related to literature, is to use a Beginning Middle End format. To do this a legal or big book size paper is folded in three vertical columns. In left to right progression each column is labelled Beginning Middle End. Students individually, in partners or in groups may select vocabulary that is important to the text. The words are written on word cards, and then sorted as to which event or character was introduced at each portion of the story. This allows the teacher a quick and effective way to determine students' comprehension and sequencing skills as they relate to the story. This can then be used as a basis for a summary or response write.

These strategies provide immediate feedback opportunities for the students, by making peer and teacher input promptly available. The interactive nature encourages listening and speaking skills as well as a level of respect for opinions and ideas.

Punctuation

Printing the punctuation on blank word cards incorporates punctuation into the students' word card writing. Students may print periods in red, commas in orange, quotation marks in green, question marks in blue etc.

Adding punctuation at this early stage in a cooperative learning environment provides practice and peer-to-peer teaching and support.

The colour coding provides rich visual clues for your students. It is great fun to have students use coloured felt pens to add correct punctuation on your shared writing charts.

Word Card Sequences

This is a list of the basic forms of words introduced. This does not include suffixes or colour words.

I

can run, play, swing, slide, hide, ride, dance, skate

see [a] boy, girl, cat, dog, park, house, school, swings, tree

like slides, bike, motorcycle cats, dogs, pets, bikes, movies, games, computers, soccer, dancing, drawing

(plurals)

a the and to
saw went was
big little
I am
(introduce **'ing'** endings)
going
in
on
fast
it
she – he –him –her
we – they
look
at
home
me – them
for
is – are
were
there – here

come – came
will

you
with
learned
tried
have – had
want
did
said
will
fun
could
would
ask
asked

Tips

Word Spacing

Often, young children do not recognize spaces between words. Using the word cards presented here creates the physical separation that the students can see. This assists them in transferring the spacing to their pencil and paper printing. You may have the students copy the Making Sentences cards onto a sentence strip that can be glued into a personal reader or class book. You may also choose to have your students copy directly into a book format.

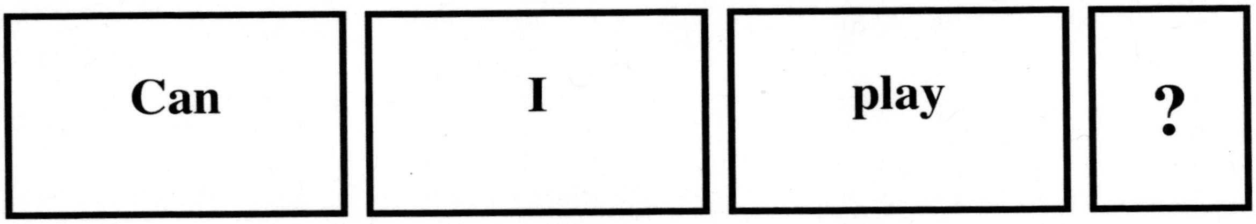

Student Responsibility – With Making Sentences students are encouraged to take responsibility to solve their own problems. For example, if a child loses a word card – the solution is that he/she obtains a blank card and copies the lost word from a learning buddy. If a student wants a personal word, he/she simply obtains a coloured blank word card and prints it with or without the help of a peer or teacher.

Blackline Masters may be enlarged on a photocopier if you assess that your students need larger manipulatives. Phrase and sentence strips may be copied onto legal size paper to create longer strips.

Double Sided Cards

Many of the words already introduced can be used in a dual format. Using double-sided cards students can increase the variety of the sentence formats. Revisiting the word card **'Can'** and making sure it has a capital form on the double-sided card is a valuable addition to question making.

"Can you come to play?" she asked.

"Can I ride the bike?" asked Jess.

"Can you see me?" Jen asked.

Look, See, Will, We, She, He, They, Can, Run, Here, There, You, Come, may all be used in lower case or upper case.

I looked at the dog.
Look at the cat run.

The boy can see the bike.
See, I can ride the big bike.

She will learn to ride.
Will the boy learn to ride?

Run to the park.
The dog can run fast.

You can play with me.
I can play with you.

Here I go.
Come here.

They can come and play.
Will they come?

There they go.
Will you go there?

By revisiting these words it allows students to continually practice them. Using them in these ways also increases their understanding of the words and their understanding of sentence structure.

Adding Vocabulary

At this point in the Making Sentences program your students have worked with over 60 basic words plus many personal words they have requested. The introduction sequence of Making Sentences words is on page 33. In addition to those words, they have added ending such as: s, es, ed, ing er and est. You have taught them about different tenses, plural matching, adjectives and adverbs. You have also taught them about sentence formation, statements and questions. Your students will no longer need to be confined to theme words.

Presenting more high frequency words is the next assignment. Introducing three to five new high frequency words during lessons will add to your students vocabulary and will add elements to their writing. Using the same format of word card introduction and games will allow your students to increase their vocabulary with more ease. Adding these words to the classroom word wall creates availability for the students.

Adding other location and activity words further enhances their reading and writing experiences. Adding in the movie theatre, school, community center, or ice-rink can create entirely new writing opportunities that use many of the words the students have already mastered. This provides valuable practice to solidify and strengthen skills.

Older students would benefit from vocabulary exposure in literature and content areas. Pre-reading and pre-writing can be supported by the use of word cards games and activities.

Materials Needed

Materials needed for Making Words are simple and readily available. The costs involved are minimal. The teacher will need:

an envelope or re closable plastic baggie for word card storage labelled with the child's name

an exercise book with a second envelope glued horizontally inside the front cover to hold homework word cards

small word cards approximately 5cm by 3cm

flip strips and the flip portion are found on page 101. You may choose to enlarge them on your photocopier

letter sized paper for Personal Books and Mini Books

letter sized paper for sentence copy strips

regular size tissue boxes with open tops to hold 'hands' of cards

- *optional storage idea – plastic binder inserts with openings for collector cards/photos or business card holders.*

Organization/Storage

It is important to select words that the students can link to their experiences.

Other general topics you could brainstorm for could be; things at an amusement park, things on a fieldtrip, a family holiday, a camping trip, a day at the beach, a snowy adventure, a visit to another planet, or visit to a farm. The topics are open to anything you and your students can create together. It is important however, to select words that the students can link to their experiences.

Chosen words are printed on small cards by the teacher and photocopied for the children. The children will print their names or initials on the back of each card and then store them in their word card envelopes or re closable baggies inside their desks. These simple words can be illustrated, read, arranged and matched to help the child learn to identify these words. Making sentences provides scaffolding for students as they begin to write their own sentences. This is a wonderful way to model writing.

Black line master of cards are provided in the master section of this manual on page 98.

I	can	ride

Another storage idea is to keep word cards in the plastic collector card pages used for collector/trading cards, or business card holders. Having students put their name or initials on the back of each word card helps in organization.

All word cards assigned by the teacher should be on one colour paper; I suggest **white**. Individual words that a child has requested should be printed on a different colour paper so they can be removed when playing the Dive In game (p.60) which requires matching. All colours of cards may be used in the Sentence Matching activity. (p.58)

Wads of Words

Don't worry your students will not be filling their desks with word cards. Create a student dictionary in a one-inch binder or scrapbook. Have students glue words in on the appropriate pages to access whenever they need to. Word dictionaries can be used to share and compare words with classmates. When they become a part of everyday use, they become used.

These learned words might also be kept in plastic card collector pages and used to play alphabetical order games. If you don't choose to create dictionaries the students may take the word cards home to share and practice with their families.

I prefer thin binders for dictionaries because extra pages may be added with ease. This also is user friendly for students who are still printing in a larger format.

Learning Activities

The following section outlines each of the activities and games used in Making Sentences program.

Making Sentences – the Word Cards

The foundation of this program is the use of high frequency, sight and phonetic word cards to make sentences that students can relate to their own experiences. Using a few words initially selected by the teacher, the teacher prints the words on the word card master sheet and photocopies word card for the students. The students will arrange the word cards to create sentences. These word card sentences can then be combined and extended to stretch development and stimulate interest.

The simplicity or complexity of sentences the children create will depend on the individuals involved. It is most effective to group words together so the children find themselves writing about a common topic. The examples I have listed in this manual are from the general topic of **<u>things to do and see at a park</u>**. The teacher chooses the topic such as 'the park' and the students brainstorm all the things to see and do at a park. Then the teacher selects some of the words to use with the first three sentence starters. For the purpose of example the words selected from the **'park' theme** are as follow: **run, play, hide, ride, see, girl, boy, cat, dog, tree, park, slide, swing** and **bike.** To begin, the teacher will choose the first simple starter and words such as:

I can play   or   I can run   or   I can ride

To begin working with the selected word cards play Show Me Tell Me (p.56) with just these 5 words. The teacher may draw students' attention to initial, medial and final sounds, rhyming [word families], letter blends, vowels and consonant sounds and variations.

For example, in the sentence 'I can run' the teacher has the opportunity to ask the children to hold up the word card that begins with the 'hard c – k' sound that has been demonstrated. The teacher may also use rhyming to help identify words. The teacher may ask the children to hold up the word card that sounds like 'fun'. Word families can be visited while introducing the selected focus words thus increasing vocabulary and word familiarity.

Now familiar with these words the teacher will model how to arrange a sentence, and ask the students to match and create the same sentence on their desktops with their word cards. These sentences can be modeled with just these 5 words.

I can run.
I can play.
I can swing

Using magnetic word cards the teacher may demonstrate a sentence and have students recreate the sentence on their desktops. This provides practice for the students to transfer information from the 'chalkboard' to their desktop, word to word matching and sequencing. Students may 'play' with magnetic word cards as a literacy activity.

When students are comfortably familiar with the selected words, more of the 'park theme' words can be introduced. This creates a foundation upon which to build all the other sentence starters. Additional sentence starters are introduced progressively throughout this program to create variety and more advanced sentence formation.

Games, cloze, poems, story frames, mini books are just a few of the activities the teacher may choose from to reinforce the sentence starter that has been introduced. Details on these activities follow.

Learning Activities – to complement sentence starters

Sentence Flip Strips

When the teacher is confident that the child can identify these words, the child is asked to put them together to make a sentence. For example, on an **'I can' strip** - the word **'run'** is printed on the flip portion and matched with a child created illustration to provide support in recalling the word. **Sentence Flips Strips** with illustrations is a fun way to support reading and sentence formation skills. Flip strips masters are found on page 101. The teacher can photocopy the beginning of the sentence onto letter size paper and then cut the strips out lengthwise. The flips are stapled on to the end of the sentence. The children print a word and illustrate it on the flip. The number of flips depends on the words the child chooses to use. An example of a student's flip may include – **I can** run-see-play-hide-slide

Using a heavier paper for the flip strips makes it sturdier and easier for the children to hold. The flips need only to be lightweight paper stapled onto the sentence end portion of the strip.

Sentence starter is printed onto the Flip Strip

The Flips are stapled on and the children print the word and illustrate

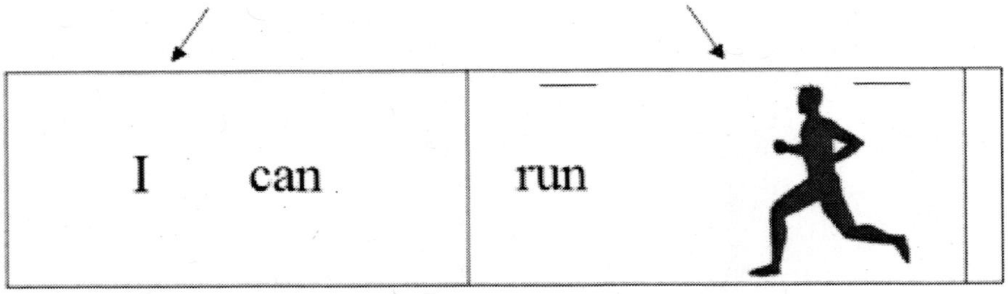

When completed, this is a quick and easy way to provide readable material for the child to share. These may be kept in a class-reading basket or sent home to join the home library.

Flip strips are very effective in this program because it provides several sentences of writing without being too labour intensive. As the fine motor control develops the teacher may choose additional or alternative activities to provide more written practice. An exercise book can be used for writing sentences. Personal books provide an activity to further increase student writing (p.46)

Mini Books

Teachers can make mini books to reinforce the vocabulary being used. The teacher simply prints the sentences on the unfolded letter size paper. Then fold the letter size paper into quarters, by first folding the top down then the left side over to create a 'card' effect. Then staple the mini book on the fold on the left. Cut the top folded edges of the mini book so all the pages can open. Due to the folding process the teacher must print the sentence starters upside down on the top quarters and right side up on the bottom quarters. This is done on both sides of the paper. See the example to determine how the position the sentences. The teacher may use mini books to introduce vocabulary, practice sentences or with sentence starters the students complete and illustrate.

Mini Books

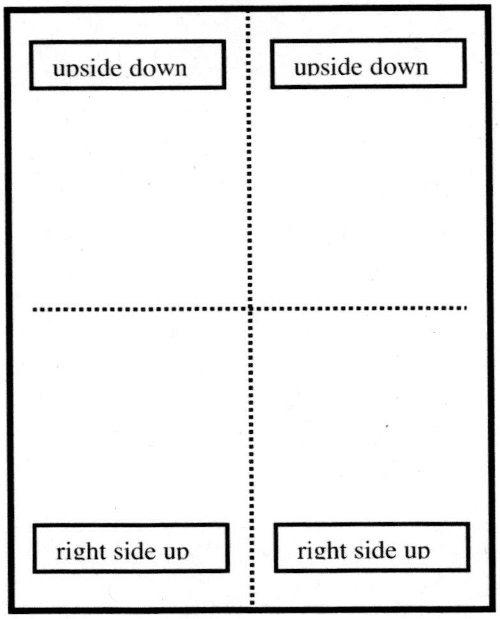

A sampling of mini books based on the first 3 sentence starters in this program is available as black line masters located in the master's section beginning on page 91.

Complete packages of Mini Books can be ordered at
www.peterson-jensica.com

Word Display Walls – the Making Sentences Way

Word walls (Cunningham 1995) are designed to provide scaffolded learning for early readers and writers. Integrating the word wall with Making Sentences and all the Making Sentences activities creates a constant connection to the words. Students are able to immerse themselves in their own vocabulary.

The Making Sentences Words the students are using are alphabetically posted on a wall for easy reference. After this initial introduction, other requested words and frequent use words can be added. An example based on the 'Park Theme' words may look like this…

A	**B**	**C**	**D**	**E**	
a	big	can	dog		
and	bike	cat			
	boy				
F	**G**	**H**	**I**	**J**	
	girl	hide			
K	**L**	**M**	**N**	**O**	
	like				
	little				
P	**Q**	**R**	**S**	**T**	
park		ride	see	the	
pet		run	slide	to	
play			swing	tree	
U	**V**	**W**	**X**	**Y**	**Z**

Word displays such as this can also be used as a literacy center by having students re-sort words or as skills develop they can begin to do simple alphabetical order, such as placing the words **ride, boy** and **park** in order.

Writing Extensions – Personal Books

Personal Books are free writing opportunities for the students. They may use the support of their word cards, classroom word displays or use invented spelling. Students, needing a new word, may print it on a blank word card if they choose to do so. To make **Personal Books** take 2 or 3 pieces of plain letter sized paper, fold in half horizontally and staple. Sentences are created with first with cards, then **copied** onto **Small Sentence Strips**, cut out of regular letter size paper [approximately 21cm across] The sentence strips are then glued into the booklet to create **Personal Books.** Children illustrate to match the sentences. These Personal Books can be added to the class reading baskets or to send home for family enjoyment. For more prolific writers the teacher simply staples 2 or 3 pages together to form a book suitable for each child or add more strips to each page.

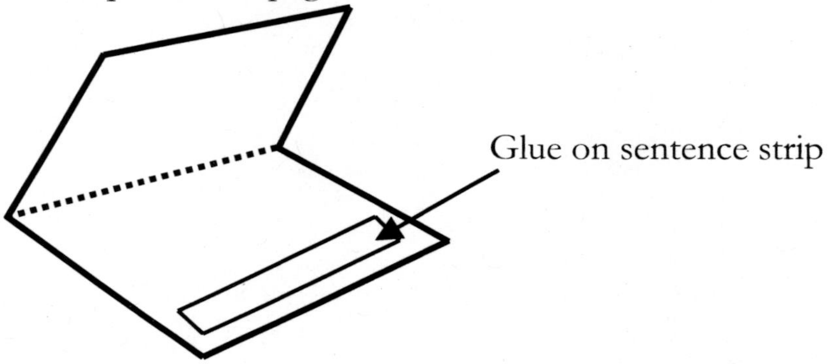

Personal books may be used in place of flip strips as students' physical writing capabilities develop.

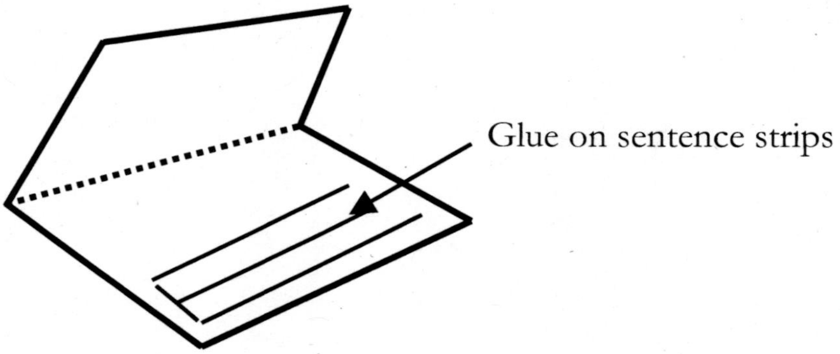

Write and Read books

Home support is indispensable in reinforcing and building upon emerging reading and writing skills. Word cards can easily be sent home in an envelope that is attached to the inside of a half plain/half-interlined exercise book called their **Write and Read Book**. This book becomes a **homework book** that provides student practice and informs parents of their child's learning and allows them an easy and fun way to be involved in that learning.

Each day that the teacher chooses to send the homework book, those word cards are put in the envelope. The homework requires the following steps:

- Children arrange the word cards in as many different sentences as they can on a tabletop or work area.
- The parent's job is to print the sentence the child has chosen into the homework book for the child. The adult's neat printing provides the child with a reading selection to practice.
- The child then copies that sentence in his/her own printing on the line below and then illustrates the sentence.

As the student's capabilities increase the parent may print in two sentences for the child to copy. As the year goes on, the teacher and parent may decide when the parent can transfer from writing to overseeing the student doing all of the sentence writing.

The **Write and Read Book** is returned the next day and becomes a part of the daily class reading activities. The teacher may wish to have children read their parent written sentences as part of their reading lesson, literacy centers or during personal reading time. Parent involvement, personal writing, choosing favourite sentences, illustrating, and reading to others makes this **Write and Read** homework activity a very valuable tool.

- A parent letter is included to begin the homework program (p.111).

Diagrams and Cartoons

At these early stages students communicate a great deal through their own use of illustrations. They also rely on illustrations to assist them in gathering meaning from written text.

Diagrams – having students create pictures about your chosen 'theme' for words. Children working with the park theme would create pictures about a park with which they are familiar. They would then label the parts of their picture with Making Sentence words. Labelling draws attention to vocabulary and descriptive terms as students focus on the diagrams and illustrations (Baskwill). Diagrams and labelling can be a more powerful tool than vocabulary lists (Moline).

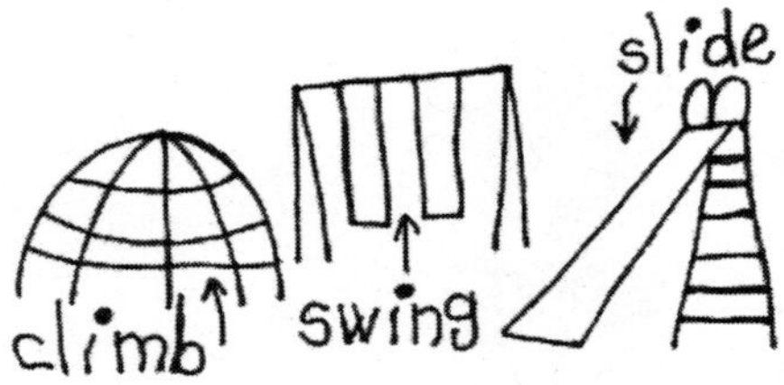

Cartoons - Children enjoy reading and creating cartoons. This is a wonderful opportunity to have students illustrate activities at the park and create talking or thinking bubbles with sentences. Older students become very engaged in cartoon creation. Cartoons can be created as a free choice activity or as a way of taking on a point of view from a literary character, or even as a content area identity or object.

Class Story Books

Create class storybooks by choosing a sentence starter and having each child contribute a page personalized with his/her own name.

For instance an "I can …" book could contain pages such as:

> Jess can ride at the park.
> Jen can swing.
> Tanner can run and hide.
> Dale can play at the park.

Another class book could be titled "We like…"

> Talia likes to play.
> Jess likes to hide.
> Larry likes to run and run at the park.

Your class books can offer variety of sentence formation as in the examples above or you may standardize each line for ease of pattern recognition for early readers. Such standardized lines may read like this:

> Jess can ride.
> Jen can swing.
> Tanner can run.

The choice in format is up to you and your students.

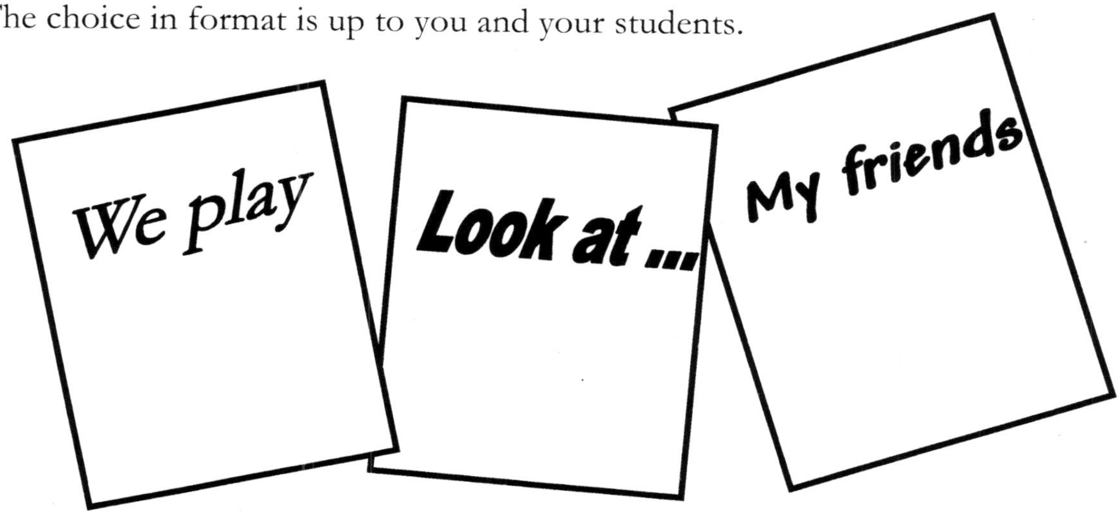

Eloquent Expression

Just as beginning students may collect words and organize them in a dictionary, older or more advanced students may collect pictures for their minds. Students may collect delicious details, fantastic phrases or mind pictures. Teachers are forever choosing material to read to their students that evoke emotions, thought or mind pictures. For instance, when I am reading to my students I keep sticky notes with me. When I read something that intrigues a student that student simply raises his/her hand and I put the sticky note on that page. After reading the student comes to the book and records the phrase they wanted to keep.

Students record these delicacies into an exercise book and keep it in their writing folders to access when writing. This extends their vocabulary and creates a sense of anticipation for the students. Adverbs and adjectives may also be colour coded with highlighters to help students when they are looking for descriptive language to use.

At times, we pull out these exercise books for an art activity, choosing an expressive phrase to illustrate or paint. The phrases can also become themes for poetic expression. Help your students yearn for the magic of literature, the art of language and transfer it into their own writing.

Treasure Detectives

Use those incredibly descriptive books that you and your students enjoy to become treasure detectives. Read stories and have the students assist you in selecting phrases and words that are delicious or exciting or enthralling or suspenseful. Record these treasures on cards or phrases to be placed in a treasure box at the writing center.

Another way of finding treasures is to use overheads to show a particularly interesting picture. Choosing illustrations from different themes create opportunities for varied descriptive language opportunities.

'Adverbs and Verbs, Adjectives and Nouns' can be printed onto cards or marked with coloured highlighters and sorted so the students are the ones to discover how and where they are used in sentences. Colour coding these parts of speech helps students make these connections. When they make the discoveries, they remember the experience.

Journal Writing

Journal writing can be supported with the incorporation of word cards. Invented writing is encouraged and valued. Confidence grows from practice and risk taking.

Sentence matching and sentence scrambles can all be used in journals. Students may be encouraged to 'keep record' of all the sentences they can make with the word cards by printing the sentences in their journals. Students see this as 'keeping score' rather than writing sentences in a book. Covertly, the teacher sets this idea in motion and smiles as the students write on their own accord.

Older students may establish their own challenge games based on sentence recording. They may work together in groups to gain points towards a preset goal. Let the students be creative and design their own motivators.

Students may also graph sentence creation results, therefore linking skill areas.

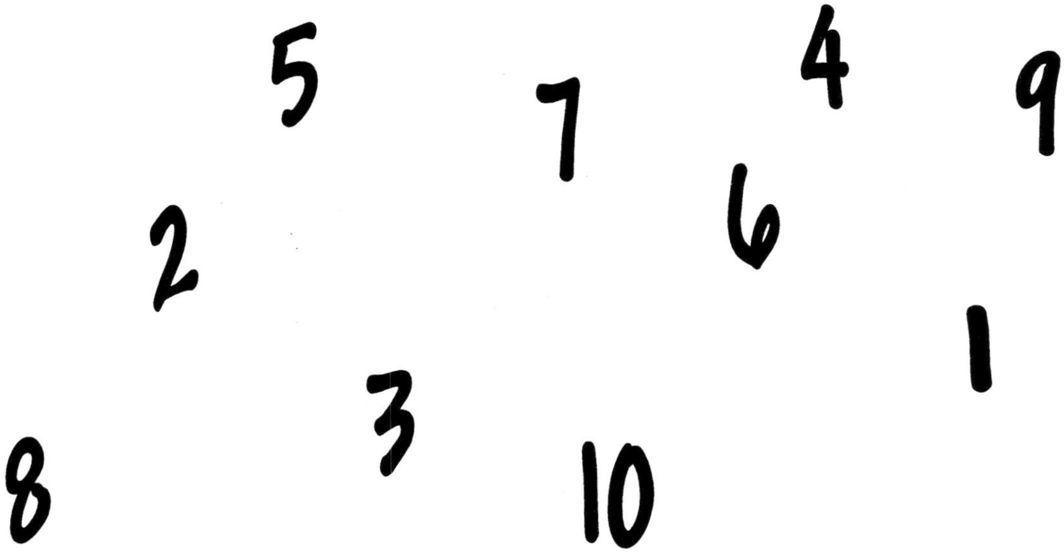

Cloze

Clozes allow students to focus in on consonant sounds, letter combinations, vowel sounds, memory, word configuration and word endings. Clozes also provide the teacher with valuable information on the mastery and usage of various reading skills. The following closes have been prepared in a paired format to enable the teacher to use them in a variety of ways. The clozes have been organized to follow the same sequence of word introduction as the Making Sentences program. Each cloze has 3 paragraphs, it is the teacher's choice to use the clozes as they appear or to copy portions of each cloze to best fit the students' needs.

First – providing paired formats and having students refer back to the non-cloze sentences to help them complete the cloze. This promotes matching correspondence and re-reading.

Second – copy only the cloze portion and assist students in using their developing skills to complete the cloze.

Third – the teacher may copy the cloze onto an overhead transparency or copy it out on a large sheet of chart paper and complete it with the children.

Blackline masters of clozes have been prepared for teachers to use with their students. You may enlarge them on a photocopier to meet the comfort of your students.

Graphing

Making Sentences transfers easily to use in graphing. The sentence starters make wonderful topics to graph. This creates even more links to reading, writing and experience.

I like...

cats	**dogs**	**rabbits**	**hamsters**	**birds**

After graphing the teacher can use a shared writing technique to help the students write about their observations on the graph. Once again connecting the writing to a purpose and communicating information.

Making Sentences from Phrases

So often students respond to questions by answering in phrases. First, the teacher can simply write the beginning of the answer on a strip. Secondly the teacher has the student highlight or underline the words from the question that are present in the beginning portion of the answer. Thirdly, the student puts the teacher portion and their own phrase answer together to form a grammatically and structurally correct sentence. By physically identifying the words reused from question to answer and by moving the two strips together the student 'sees, hears, and kinaesthetically' learns how a sentence is formed. This would only be done for the students who need this scaffolding and would only be provided until the student is able to transfer to independent writing. When the student 'relapses' the teacher may show 2 blank strips to the student as a reminder.

as shadows danced

sunshine smiling

like a feather on a breeze

Poem Detectives

Prepare individual poem sheets in addition to pocket charts or large class size poems. Have the students mark the rhyming words in the following poems. The teacher may have students mark the rhymes by asking them to circle or box or underline or colour the matching rhymes on their poem sheets.

Putting these poems on sentence strips in a pocket chart or writing it on a chart and searching for the rhyming words together is effective in teaching about word endings and introducing new words in the poem.

Fun

I like to play
in the sun
all day
it
is
fun!

After focusing on rhyming words, the teacher may ask the students to mark or colour specific words. For example a teacher may say find the word that has a vowel ' i ' that says I (like). Another example is to ask the students to find the word that ends with the ' t ' sound. The things a teacher focuses on will depend on the skills being taught at that time.

This poem detective activity promotes listening skills and particularly following directions. Vocabulary can be introduced such as; underline, circle, box, before, after, etc. when referring to the target words in the poem.

Learning Games

Learning games provide the needed rehearsals to commit learning to memory. Games also grasp and maintain students attention. By using games your students develop literacy, communication and social skills necessary to be successful. In each game the elements can be extended or enhanced to match the capabilities of more advanced or older students.

Show Me Tell Me

With each new group of words to be introduced the teacher will play a word identifying game called " **Show Me Tell Me** ". Select only a small grouping of words at a time, for example, play the **Show Me Tell Me** game with the words: I – can - run - play - hide. This allows the children to become familiar with the words and leads them towards success when creating sentences. When the children demonstrate accurate recognition of the word cards, you may work with them to make sentences.

To play the game the children will spread out their word cards at their own working area (desk or table top). Then the teacher holds up one of the larger teacher cards, or prints the selected word on the board or chart, and asks the children to hold up the card that reads, 'can'. The game progresses with the children looking for and holding up each word that the teacher has held up. This practices sight word location and matching.

As the children become proficient with this game they can play it in small groups without the teacher. This game is effective if played after each new group of words is introduced.

Keep in mind, that individual students may ask for 'special' words in addition to the selected words the teacher has introduced. Special request words are printed on a different colour word cards stock so they can be used or separated depending on the activity.

- Larger word cards used by the teacher are easily made by using the enlarging option on a photocopier.
- If you attach magnets or use magnetic paper they can easily be displayed on a magnetic board or most chalkboards and students can use them as a literacy center activity.

Troublesome Words

'Where and were' are often confused in spelling. Their, there and they're along with to, too and two can cause some trouble. Using these in the 'Show Me Tell Me' game is a fun way to practice these. The teacher will ask for students to hold up the word that means " the number two" or a word that means " too much" or "me too". For spelling confusion the teacher may call a word by using it is a sentence, such as " We were playing." This provides the visual practice coupled with the expressive meaning. Games are experiential and therefore create memories that the students can recall and utilize in reading and writing.

Read and Riddle

This game is best played with older students in partners or groups. Word cards are placed in a bag or box, turns are taken to select a word and provide clues until the word is guessed. For example, if the word 'treasure' was selected a student may say " pirates make maps for this " or " it is in a chest". Students gain points for the number of clues they can provide for each word and the guessing students gain a point for guessing the word. To track points students may take a popsicle stick for each point. Then the points can be calculated at the end of the game. The end of the game can be set at a predetermined amount of points or words or as time allows.

Sentence Matching

This **Sentence Matching** activity is best done in pairs. All you will need is the word card envelopes for each child, a pencil and a small amount of blank cards. Children may work together, with one child creating a sentence with their word cards, then the partner matches it with their word cards. When the children come to a word that only one of them has, the other child simply makes a new card and uses it immediately. That child may keep the new word or may recycle it after the game. **Sentence Matching** is a fun and independent activity that children can do successfully while the teacher is working with another student or with a small group. All colours of word cards can be used in this game.

The teacher will need to have a supply of blank white and coloured word cards available.

* Photo Album pages with the sticky surface and the flip over acetate cover are wonderful for the students to use as a working surface for Making Sentences. Students can place word cards on the album page, flip the plastic cover down and show the completed writing to a peer or teacher without needing to worry about spilling them.

Sentence Scramble

The Sentence Scramble game is played with a partner. Each player makes a sentence with the word cards. They read each other's sentences, trade them and then mix them up and put the words back into the correct sentence order. For example, Tanner chooses his word cards to create the sentence

'I can see a motorcycle.'

Then Lauren chooses her word cards for the sentence

' I like to play.'

They trade card sentences, read them, scramble them up and assemble them in the correct order again. Each of the partners provides help and confirmation as their own sentence is recreated.

Students enjoy the individuality and control over their own sentence creation. The confidence that is gained by each child who is able to help a classmate is very valuable.

As in the Sentence Matching game, all colours of word cards may be used. Students simply create a new card to use in the sentences if their partner has a 'special' word that they did not yet have.

When introducing these games the teacher may choose to have the students use their own word cards or may choose to have a basic set of word cards available at that literacy center area.

Dive In

Dive In can only be played after the children have been introduced to several words to allow for enough cards to be placed in the 'Dive In' bag. The Dive In bag can be any kind of paper or fabric bag. Only use the teacher assigned word cards that have been printed on white paper. The special request word cards will create a matching problem if used in this game.

Dive In is a word card game similar to 'Go Fish'. Children play in groups of 2 to 6. They do not have to be paired off. Each player takes only 3 cards out of the Dive In Bag. Each player looks at their cards and tries to find a match either in their hand or by asking one fellow player "Do you have the card **run**?" If the player asked does have the card they give it to the requesting player. If the player asked does not have the card they say 'Dive In' and the player reaches into a paper bag to access the remaining word cards. The card that is pulled out becomes a part of that player's hand of cards. When players have a matched pair of word cards, they place them to their side. Players can only lay down paired cards at the beginning of their turn. The game ends when all the cards have been used from the Dive In bag. The winner is the player with the most word card pairs.

An extension for older or more capable students is to play 'Dive In' by asking for a word that means… or a word that rhymes with… or a word that is opposite of... Changing the details of the game allows students the comfort of a known format but challenges them to think of other ways to describe and interact with words.

Contractions

Playing a matching concentration game with contractions is a quick and fun way to expose the students to a variety of new words. Copy contractions onto a coloured paper (a different colour for each set of cards). These contraction cards can be kept at a literacy or game center so you will only need 2 to 4 sets. Students will take one set of contraction cards and spread them out upside down. Then students take turns flipping two cards over, if the words match to a contraction the student gets to keep the cards. When all the cards have been matched the game is over and each player counts up the cards to see who won.

A blackline master for this game can be found on page 110.

Compound Words

Compound words can be taught in the same way as Contractions by using a matching game. Set of 'playing cards' may be copied off and stored at a literacy or game center. Students gain points by counting all the new words they made. For extra points they can be illustrated or used in sentences.

Certain compound words make funny pictures when taken literally. Have students make displays showing a 'mailman' or a 'watchdog' or a 'catfish'

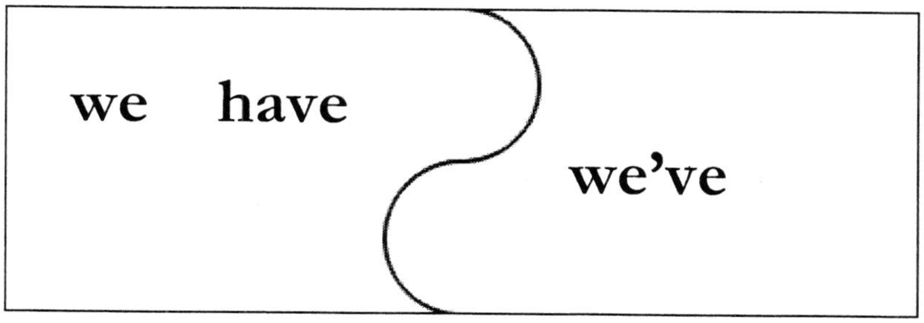

A blackline master can be found on page 110.

Rhyme It – card game

These rhyming cards are based upon the word cards you have introduced throughout this program. Choose a special colour paper for the rhyming word cards. These cards would be kept separate from student cards.

Prepare a tissue box for each player as a cardholder. Each player takes 5 cards from the 'face down' pile. These 5 cards are placed face up inside the tissue box. This allows young children to easily see each card. The child can easily compare the letter endings in the words to help determine if it is a rhyming match or not. Players take turns asking for a card that rhymes with one of their cards (Can you rhyme with **tan**?). If a match is found the lucky player puts the rhyming cards together 'face up' beside their tissue box. Then that player must take a new card from the pile. (5 cards need to be in play throughout the game). If no match is made the play moves to the next player. When the extra card pile has been used up the players may ask for and match to the cards in players' tissue boxes. When a child has a card that rhymes with cards already matched the player may add to the match. This created a rhyming word family of cards.

Below is an example of rhyming cards based on a few of the original words used in the first sentence starters. You may select any grouping of rhyming words suitable for your children.

can -	ban Dan fan man pan ran tan van
run -	bun fun gun sun
play -	bay day hay lay may pay ray say way stay
swing -	bring cling ding fling ping ring sing wing
hide -	ride side tide wide slide
see -	be free he she me tree we
cat-	at bat fat hat mat pat rat sat flat
dog -	bog fog frog hog log
park -	bark dark lark mark
like -	bike hike Mike

These cards and tissue boxes may be kept with other learning centers. The teacher may use this game as a literacy center, a general center time activity or as a spare time activity.

This game requires each child to focus on the sounds in the words as well as the look of the words. It is a fun and easy way to provide decoding and sight word practice. This game may be played with 2 to 4 players. Each teacher must determine the appropriate time to introduce this game.

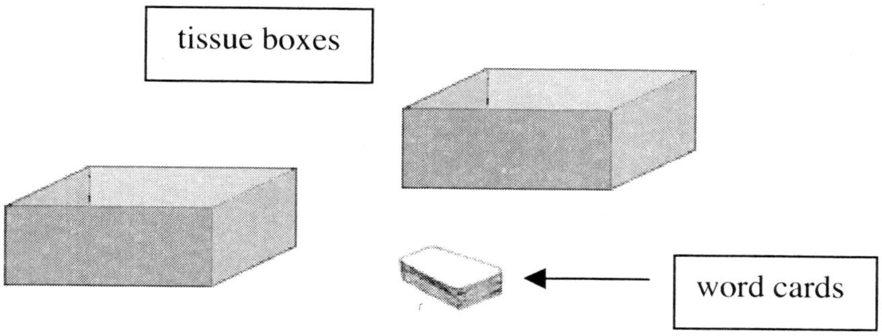

The teacher may cut off the top of regular sized tissue boxes to serve as cardholders. The students place their cards in the bottom of the box rather than trying to hold the cards in their hands. The box provides privacy for the players 'hand'.

The following word families are from words introduced with future sentence starters.

he -	be he me she we
look-	book cook hook took
came-	blame fame game name same tame
will-	Bill fill gill hill mill pill still till will
park-	bark dark lark Mark
see -	bee free tree agree
and -	band hand land sand
am -	clam ham Pam ram Sam

Drama

As we all know, movement with learning helps children assimilate and retain their learning. Making Sentences easily allows for kinesthetic involvement.

Student Charades

Prepare sentence strips such as; I can run – I can hide I can ride a bike etc. and help the students take turns acting them out.

The actor will take a sentence out of a bag to read and perform, while the audience members look at the possible sentences arranged in front of them. When an audience member believes he/she knows the sentence being demonstrated he/she holds up the correct sentence strip. This format requires each student to read the sentence strips, creating fun practice.

Sentence Cubes

The teacher will print a sentence starter such as; 'I can …' on a strip and place in front of the players. Then using a black line master for a cube the teacher will print words such as; – jump – run – sing – sit – hide – ride on the cube. Then students will roll the cube and take turns acting out the sentence.

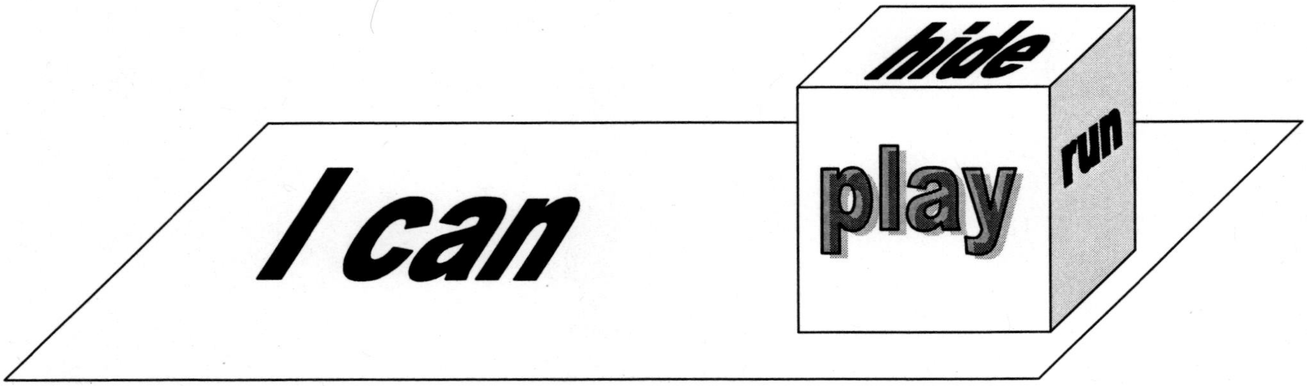

Instead of Said

Playing games with conversational writing provides fun exploration; creativity and practice in correct speaker identification in writing and develops expression and fluency in oral reading. This is very valuable for your older or more capable students.

Using two different colour strips of paper the students use word cards and/or invented spelling to write the content of what a character is saying, then on the other colour strip the speaker identification is written.
Step One - Brainstorm alternate ways to say "said" or and post these is an easily visible location in your classroom.

Step Two - For example, on the blue strip the student writes " Are we there yet?"

Step Three - On the yellow strip the student writes **whined** followed by a blank name area; e.g. **whined _______________.**

Step Four - After the group of students has created their strips the strips presented to the rest of the group/class. Once everyone has an idea of the content the game begins.

Step Five - All the blue conversation strips are placed in one bag. All the yellow speaker strips are placed in a second bag.

Step Six – Now the students take turn taking a strip from each bag. Each student takes their strips and goes with a partner to practice their two strips. Each child helps the other practice the conversational strip using the type of voice expression recorded on the other strip.

For example, if a child selects **" It was an accident"** and the strip that said **giggled _____________.** The partner may have selected **" I like pizza"** and the strip that said **shouted _____________.** Each student helps each other read and practice the strips.

Step Seven – The students perform their sentence using vocal expression to make the conversational statement or question 'sound' as the speaker identification indicated.

The 'Instead of Said' game promotes expression and fluency in oral reading. This activity also provides practice using colourful language that they can then transfer into their writing. I have included a partial list of 'said substitutes'.

agreed
argued
asked
babbled
barked
bawled
begged
bellowed
blurted
boasted
bubbled
bugged
clucked
cheered
chuckled
coaxed
commanded
complained
coughed
cried
croaked

dared
demanded
exclaimed
fussed
fumed
gasped
gulped
giggled
growled
hinted
hissed
hollered
howled
joked
laughed
lied
moaned
mumbled
nagged
praised
promised

protested
questioned
ranted
roared
snarled
snickered
sniffed
snorted
sobbed
squeaked
stormed
shrieked
suggested
teased
told
warned
wept
whispered
whined
yawned
yelled

Another activity that created visual memory connections is illustrated printing.

Illustrated printing is when the student selects a word and prints it using letter shapes and styles that depict the actual word. Students may even add picture details around the word to provide more connection opportunities.

joked

whined

SHRIEKED

SHOUTED

whispered

Ping-Pong Panic

Ping Pong Panic is a hilarious and energetic game. Student will be learning and practicing spelling skills, rhyming, word recognition, social interaction and cooperation, oral language and problem solving.

To play, the teacher will use either ping-pong balls, or the plastic ball pit balls, or plastic Easter eggs. Word family endings such as: at, ot, an, ell, ike, ide, ack, etc. can be printed in blue ink onto one third of the balls. The remaining two thirds of balls will have single consonants or consonant blends printed in red. The colour coding assists the students in matching up parts of words.

To play the game, the balls are thrown and scattered throughout the gym or large floor area. The students may work in partners or teams to run and find balls to match up to create conventionally spelled words.

This game is a favourite for students of all ages.

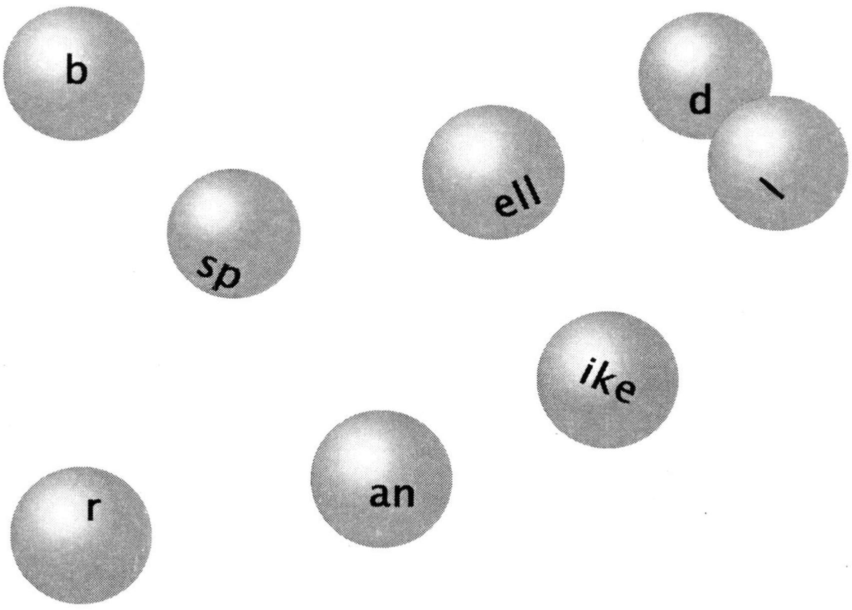

Word Families

ack - back black clack hack lack Mack lack pack rack sack tack whack
ail - bail fail mail nail pail rail sail tail
ain - gain main pain rain stain
ake - bake cake fake flake lake make rake sake take wake
ale - bale Dale gale male pale sale stale tale whale
all - ball call fall hall mall stall tall wall
ame - blame came fame flame game lame name same tame
an - ban can Dan fan man pan ran tan
ank - bank clank drank sank tank thank blank
ap - cap flap gap lap map nap sap tap strap
ash - bash cash dash flash gash lash mash rash sash stash (wash)
at - bat cat fat flat hat mat pat rat sat (what)
ate - crate date gate grate hate late mate
aw - caw draw flaw law paw raw saw
ay - bay clay day hay lay may pay ray say tray way
eat - beat cheat heat meat neat seat wheat
ell - bell fell sell tell well yell
est - best nest pest rest test west
ice - dice mice nice rice
ick - chick lick pick Rick sick stick tick
ide - bride glide hide pride ride side tide wide
ight - bright light might night right sight tight
ill - Bill fill gill hill mill pill still till will
in - bin fin pin tin thin twin win
ine - dine fine line mine nine pine
ing - bring cling ding fling ping ring sing thing wing
ink - blink clink drink link mink pink rink sink think wink
ip - blip clip chip dip flip hip lip rip sip tip trip whip
it - bit fit flit hit lit pit sit wit
ock - clock dock flock lock rock sock
og - bog cog clog dog fog hog log
old - bold cold fold gold hold mold sold told
ook - book brook cook look took
op - cop crop drop flop hop mop pop stop top
ore - core more sore store
ot - cot dot got hot lot not pot rot tot
uck - buck cluck duck luck puck suck stuck truck
ug - bug chug dug hug mug rug tug
ump - bump clump dump hump jump lump pump stump

(Wylie & Durrell 1970)

Fat Cat

It is a cat
that sat and sat
And sat and sat
And now it is fat.

Dog and Frog

The dog looked
in the bog
on the log
at the frog.

Dan Dan

Dan Dan
the tan van man
likes to sing
and like to play
drives around in
the van all day.

Hiding

Look at me
in the tree.
I can hide.
I can play.
I can see
up in the tree.

Noises

It went bling
it went cling
it went ping
And ring a ding ding.
It went wing
it went zing
it went pling a ting ting.

Poetry written by L. Peterson

Poem Frames – **based on sentence starter words**

These poems can be enlarged on a photocopier for student use or the teacher could make an overhead sheet or chart poem.

Talk

Ruff says the ____________	dog
Meow says the ____________	cat
Ribbit says the ____________	frog
And that is that.	

The Park

I can ________	
I can play	run, slide, swing, slide, hide, ride,
I can ________	
at the park all day.	

Friends

You and ______	me
He and _______	she
They and we	
All are friends.	

I Will

She could _____________	
He could_______________	run, slide, swing, slide, hide, ride,
You could _____________	see, play,
We could ______________	
But I will ______________	

Wishes

I wish I had a ____________
I wish I had a ____________
I wish I had a ____________
I wish I had a ____________
I wish I had a cat
I wish I had a purple elephant
What to you think about that?

dog, swing, park, house, bike, pet
motorcycle

Playing

Playing on the ______________
Playing on the ______________
Playing on the ______________
I like playing.

These poems can be enlarged and bound together to make class big books to support your classroom library.

Story Frames – based on sentence starters.

Story frames are another way to reinforce the reading sentences. The fill in the blank process supports reluctant writers by limiting their physical written output yet resulting in a story. Students can add miniature illustrations to help them read the stories. You may enlarge poem and story frames for student use.

For older students you can divide the class into groups and create story frames in a shared writing format. The story frames may be copied off and traded with other students to create your own "Mad Libs". Once again, because the words come from your students, they are valued, they have ownership and you have their attention. Creating story frames is an effective way of teaching tense shifts, ordinals, plurals, nouns, verbs, adverbs, adjectives even synonyms and antonyms.

At the Park

______________________ wanted to play.

______________ went to the park.

There were __________________at the park.

There were __________________ at the park.

There were boys and girls playing.

At Home

I can play at home.

I can ______________________________.

I can ______________________________.

I can ______________________________.

I like to play with ______________________________.

Fun

I like to ______________________________.

I like to ______________________________.

I like to ______________________________.

I like to ______________________________.

________________________ and I have fun.

The Park

I like to ________________at the park.

I like to see the _____________________ play.

The _________________ run.

The girls and boys ________________________.

I can see ________________ riding bikes.

I can play.

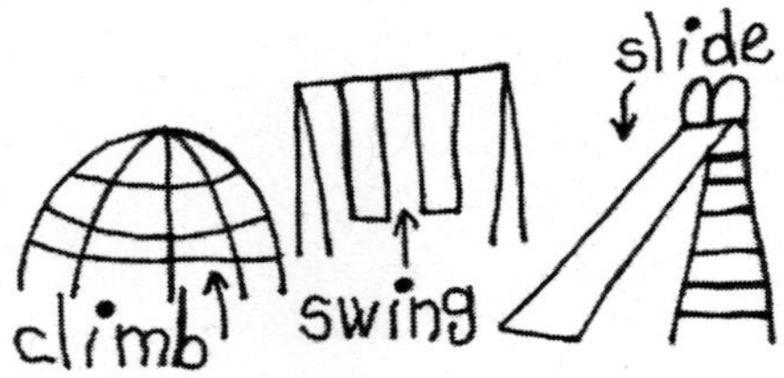

Clozes #1,2,3 after the **I like sentence starter** uses these words-
I can see like run play slide swing park
the little cat dog hide a and girl boy big
fast hide ride bike

Clozes #4,5,6 after the **I went I saw sentence starters**
uses these words – saw went was I am going fast to it

Clozes #7,8,9 after **Singular Pronoun sentence starters –**
uses these words – she he we they him her

Cloze #10,11,12 after **Look sentence starter**
uses these words – look at me for is are

Cloze #13,14,15 after There and Here sentence starters
uses these words - there here come came

Cloze #16,17,18 after **the Will You sentence starter –**
uses these words – you with will come came there here

Cloze #19,20,21 after **the I want sentence starter**
uses these words – learned tried have want did

Cloze #22,23,24 after the **I said sentence starter –**
uses these words – did said

Cloze #25,26,27 after the Questioning Sentence starters
uses these words – could would fun

Cloze #28,29,30 after Questioning Sentence starters
uses these words - ask asked

Cloze 1,2 & 3

name: ____________________

I can run and play.
I like slides and swings.
I like the park.

I see a little cat.
The cat sees a dog.
The dog runs and the cat hides.

I see a girl.
I see a boy.
The girl and boy can play.

....

I ca__ run and pl__y.
I li__e slides and swings.
I like the par__.

I se__ a little cat.
The ca__ sees a dog.
The do__ runs and the cat hides.

I __ee a girl.
I se__ a boy.
The girl and boy ca__ play.

Cloze 4, 5 & 6

____
name

I saw a little girl.
The girl was riding a bike.
The girl went to the park.

I saw a boy.
The boy was running fast.
The boy was playing.

I am going to see the dog.
I am going to pet it.
I like dogs.

....

I __aw a little girl.
The girl was ri__ing a bike.
The girl went to the par__.

I __aw a boy.
The boy was running fas__.
The __oy was playing.

I am going to see the dog.
I a__ going to pet it.
I __ike dogs.

Cloze 7, 8 & 9

____
name

She was running.
The boy was riding.
They went fast.

The little cat was playing.
She was running and hiding.
We like to pet it.

He was running to her.
She was going to hide.
They went to play.

....

She was __unning.
The __oy was __iding.
They we__t __ast.

The __ittle ca__ was playing.
She was __unning and hi__ing.
We like to __et it.

He was __unning to he__.
__he was __oing to hide.
They went to __ __ay.

Cloze 10, 11 &12

____

name

Look at me run.
I went to play at the park.
I like slides and swings.

She is looking for me.
I went to hide.
We are playing.

He went to the park.
She is going to play.
They are going to look for boys and girls.

....

L__ __k at me run.
I went to __lay at the par__.
I like slides an__ swings.

She is loo__ing fo__ me.
I wen__ to hide.
W__ are playing.

He __ent to the __ark.
She is __oing to __lay.
They are going to __ook for __oys and girls.

Cloze 13, 14 & 15

____
name

There is a boy.
Here is a girl.
They came to play.

They can come to play.
I am going to go riding.
Come and ride here.

Come here and see me.
We can run and play.
We can ride bikes.

....

There is a __oy.
__ere is a __irl.
They __ame to pl__ __.

They c__ __ come to play.
I a__ going to __o riding.
__ome and __ide here.

Come __ere and __ee me.
We c__ __ run and pl__y.
We can __ide bikes.

Cloze 16, 17 & 18

____
name

I went to play with the boys.
We went riding.
Will you come to play?

They went there to play.
We can play here.
You came to see me.

Will you play with me?
Can you come here?
I can come there.

....

I w__ n__ to play wi__ __ the boys.
We went rid__ __ __.
__ill you __ome to play?

They __ent there to pl__ __.
We c__n p__ay here.
You __ame to see me.

Will you pl__ __ with me?
Can yo__ come here?
I can __ome there.

Cloze 19, 20 & 21 ____________________ name

I learned to ride a bike.
I went riding with the boys and girls.
Did you want to come with me?

I have a little bike.
I tried to ride the big bike.
I want to learn to ride it.

Have you learned to ride?
Did you ride to the park?
The boy and girl tried to ride.

....

I lea__ned to ri__ __ a bike.
I went rid__ __ __ with boys and __irls.
Di__ you wa__t to come with me?

I __ave a little bike.
I tried to r__de the b__g bike.
I want to lea__n to ride it.

Ha__e you learned __o ride?
__id you r__de to the park?
The b__ __ and girl tried to ride.

Cloze 22, 23 &24

name

Did you learn to ride?
I tried to ride.
I did learn.

He said he can ride.
She said she can ride a big bike.
They learned to ride.

She said, "Look at me."
He said, "Look at me."
I saw the boy and girl.

D__d you __earn to ride?
I tr__ed to ride.
I __id learn.

H__ said he c__n ride.
She said sh__ can r__de a b__g bike.
__ __ey learned to ride.

__ __e said, "Loo__ at me."
He said, "L__ __k at me."
I __aw the boy __nd girl.

Cloze 25, 26 & 27

____
name

I would like to see you.
Would you like to see me?
We could go and play.

She said, "I cold come to play."
He said, "I would like to play."
They will have fun.

They could come to play.
We would have fun.
We learned to ride.

....

I woul__ like to see you.
Would yo__ like to see m__?
We could g__ and play.

__ __e said, "I c__ __ld come to play."
He said, "I would li__e to play."
They will have f__n.

They could __ome to play.
We would h__ve fun.
W__ learned to ri__e.

Cloze 28, 29 & 30

____
name

She asked him to play.
He said they could come play.
They went to swing and slide.

There is a little girl.
I will ask her to come to play.
They went to see a little dog.

A boy asked to pet the dog.
He liked the big dog.
They went running and playing.

....

She asked h__m to play.
__e said they could __ome play.
They went to __ __ing and slide.

There is a l__ttle girl.
I will __sk her to come to play.
They went to see a little d__g.

A boy ask__ __ to pet the dog.
He liked the b__g do__.
They __ent running and play__ __ __.

Word Searches

Word searches are incorporated into Making Sentences as a fun method of reinforcing word recognition skills. Included are four word searches prepared from the first group of theme words. A blank black line master is available for the teacher to create word searches for their own classroom needs.

Word searches are effective ways to practice letter sequencing, spelling, word identification and word matching. Older students may create their own word searches, proofread them and trade. The ownership of these activities promotes self-confidence as well as skill development.

____
name

Word Search #1

p a r k d g e e j k a s b e p a t r u n

d o s l l d e e a t n o t o c a n r a t h

j h a l e c d f l i k e r o n u p l s e t b i

a n d p l a y b e v g I p m o d o a z

Find the words: **park run can slide I play**

____

name

Word Search #2

p a r k d s e e j k a s b e p a t r u n

d o b i k e m e a t n o t o c a t r a

j b i g c d s w i n g o n u p n i s e t

a n s l i d e b e v g I p c a n o a z p

Find the words: **see bike swing slide I can a big**

Draw a picture to show one or two words in the word search.

name

Word Search #3

p a r k d g e e j k a s b e c a t r u n i

d o s e e m p e t s o t o c a n r a t h

j h a l e c d I l i k e r o n u p l a y t b i

a n d p l a y b d o g l p m o d o a z

Find the words: **I like pets a see can cat dog play**

Draw a picture to show one or two words in the word search.

name

Word Search #4

t h e k d g e e j k a s b e p a t r u n

d o s e e m e g i r l t o c a n r a t h

j h a I b o y f g l r l r u l i k e s e t b i

a n d p l a y b e v g l p m o d o a z

Find the words: **I like to play girl boy can the**

Draw a picture to show one or two words in the word search.

____
name

Word Search ______________________

Find these words: ______________________

____

____

____

(Gay Su Pinnell and Irene C. Fountas)

#1
I can

I can swing.

I can hide.

I can play.

I can slide.

I can run.

I can see.

I can ride.

I see a boy.

I see a girl.

#2

I can see.

I see a tree.

I see a cat.

I can see a bike.

I can see.

I see a swing.

I like boys.

I like girls.

#3 I like

I like bikes.

I like dogs.

I like swings.

I like cats.

I like rides.

Word Ending 'under lays'

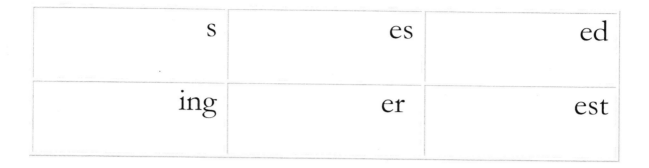

s	es	ed
ing	er	est

These cards are matched in size to the word cards so the students can place the word ending cards **under** the word cards to create the new word forms.

Another option is to copy the word card endings onto overhead sheets so they can be placed on top of the words with the endings completing the words

Endings that require the changing of ' y ' to an ' i ' can be addressed by placing the ending over the word ending so that the viewed word is correctly spelled.

Basic Word Cards – masters

Photocopy and hand out the words that you select. Children print names or initials on the back of each card and keep it in their own word envelope.

I	can	see
like	run	play
swing	hide	ride
a	boy	girl
cat	dog	tree
bike	pets	to
the	and	park

Basic word Cards – blank masters

Use these to add in your own words or the personal words that your children request. Photocopy personal words on a different colour than your class word selections. You may enlarge the cards to fit your students' needs.

When you have evidence that your students have been successful with a grouping of word cards the cards may be sent home or placed in a reference notebook to use as a writing guide. Keep extra blank white cards for the students to use to reprint any lost cards. Keep extra coloured blanks for students who want to add personal words.

Black line Master for sentence strips and use in personal books or phrase strips

These may also be used with older students to:

- assist them in creating complete sentences with the beginning and ending phrases.
- take notes for research - phrases or point form reduces plagiarism
- identifying main ideas
- recording descriptive phrases to include in writing

I can

I can

I can

I like

I like

I like

I see

I see

I see

Flips for the student illustration and word, stapled onto the Sentence Flip Strip.

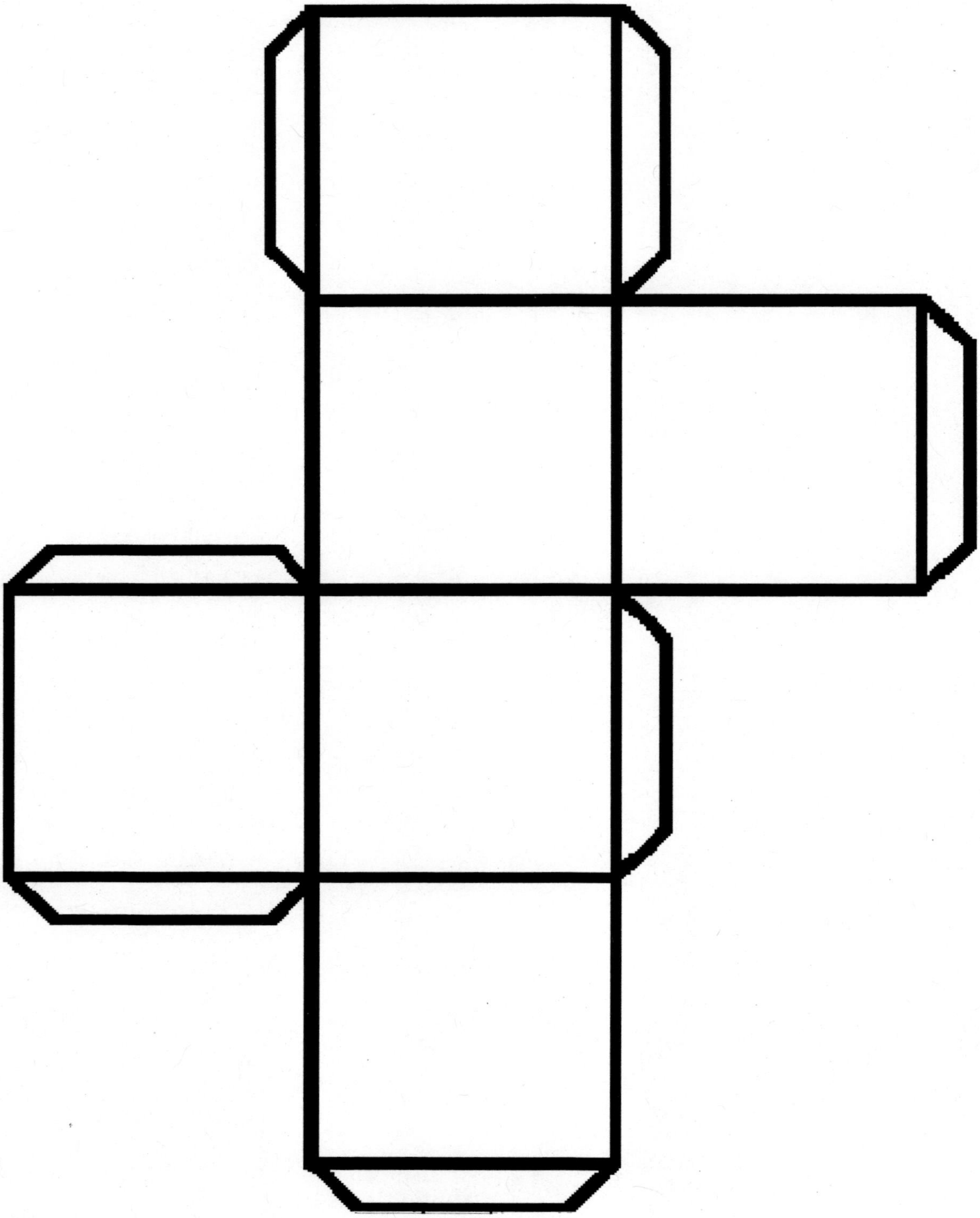

Memories

By ____________________

Contraction Word List

are not = aren't
can not = can't
could have = could've
did not = didn't
does not = doesn't
had not = hadn't
has not = hasn't
have not = haven't
he is = he's
he would = he'd
here is = here's
I am = I'm
I had = I'd
I have = I've
I will = I'll
I would = I'd
is not = isn't
it is = it's
let us = let's
might have = might've
must have = must've
she is = she's
she will = she'll
she would = she'd
should not = shouldn't
should have = should've
that is = that's
there is = there's
they are = they're
they have = they've
they will = they'll
they would = they'd
was not = wasn't
we are = we're
we have = we've
we will = we'll
we would = we'd
were not = weren't
what is = what's
who is = who's
will not = won't
would have = would've
would not = won't
you are = you're
you had = you'd
you have = you've
you will = you'll
you would = you'd

Compound Word List

Airport
Background
Backstop
Ballroom
Barnyard
Baseball
Bathroom
Bedspread
Bedtime
Breakfast
Bubblegum
Bulldog
Bullfrog
Buttercup
Butterfly
Catfish
Cottontail
Countdown
Cowboy
Cowgirl
Crossroad
Cupcake
Daybreak
Daydream
Daylight
Daytime
Dogcatcher
Dogfish
Driveway
Drumstick
Dugout
Dustpan
Earring
Endless
Evergreen
Eyeball
Eyelash
Farmhouse
Featherbed
Fingernail
Fingerprint
Firecracker
Firefly
Fireman
Firewood
Foghorn
Football
Footstep
Fingernail
Goldfish
Grandchild
Grandfather
Grandmother
Grasshopper
Gumdrop
Hairbrush
Haircut
Handshake
Handyman
Headfirst
Headache
Headlight
Headphone
Herself
Himself
Homework
Horseback
Housecoat
Inside
Itself
Jellyfish
Jigsaw
Keyhole
Kneecap
Ladybug
Leapfrog
Litterbug
Lumberjack
Mailbox
Mailman
Maybe
Mealtime
Moonlight
Motorboat
Motorcycle
Notebook
Nothing
Nowhere
Oatmeal
Outburst
Outdoor
Outfit
Outgoing
Outline
Outside
Overhead
Overjoyed
Pancake
Paperback
Paperwork
Passport
Pathway
Peephole
Pickup
Piggyback
Pigtail
Playmate
Policeman
Popcorn
Pullover
Purebred
Quicksand
Racehorse
Racetrack
Railroad
Rainbow
Raincoat
Rainfall
Rattlesnake
Roadside
Roommate
Rowboat
Runway
Sailboat
Sandbox
Sandman
Scarecrow
Schoolhouse
Seashell
Seashore
Seaweed
Shoelace
Sidewalk
Signpost
Sleepyhead
Snowfall
Snowman
Softball
Somebody
Someone
Something
Spaceship
Spiderman
Springtime
Starfish
Starlight
Summertime
Sunday
Sundown
Sunflower
Sunlight
Sunrise
Sunset
Superman
Takeoff
Teardrop
Textbook
Themselves
Thumbnail
Thunderstorm
Toothpaste
Tugboat
Underpants
Understand
Upon
Volleyball
Washroom
Watchdog
Watermelon
Weekday
Weekend
Windshield
Without
Wonderland
Yearbook
Yourself

Blackline master for compound word and contraction game cards.
The teacher may print in the selected words and copy off sets for student use.

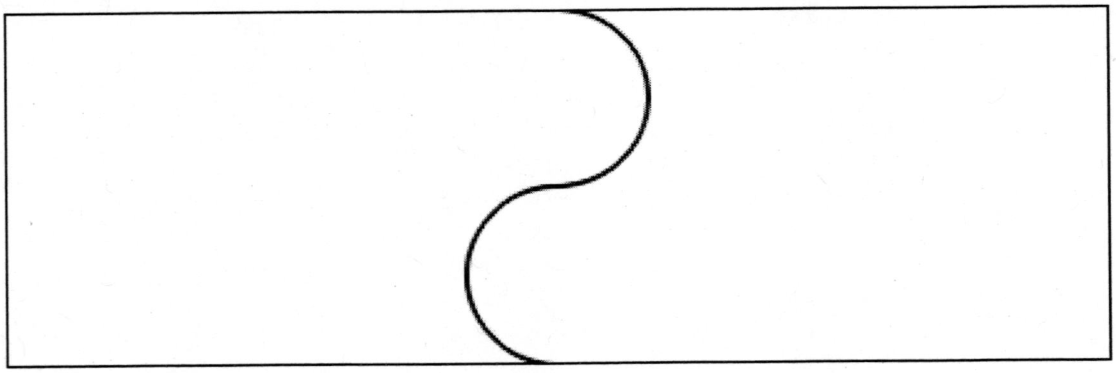

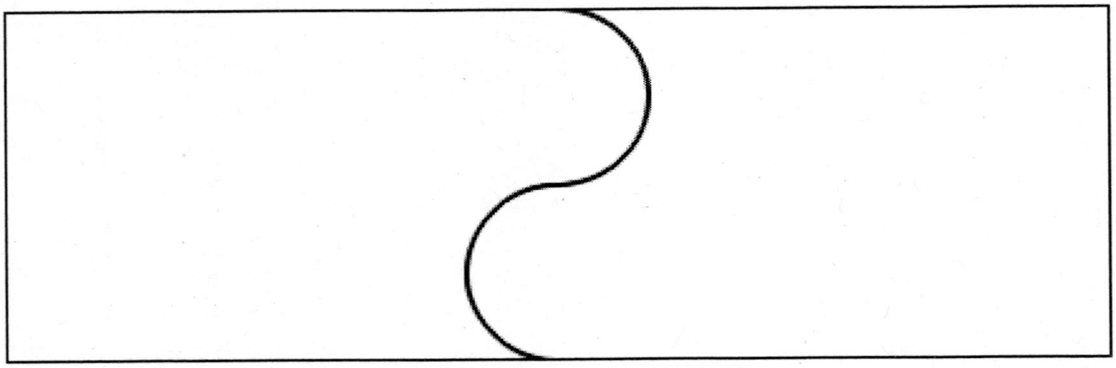

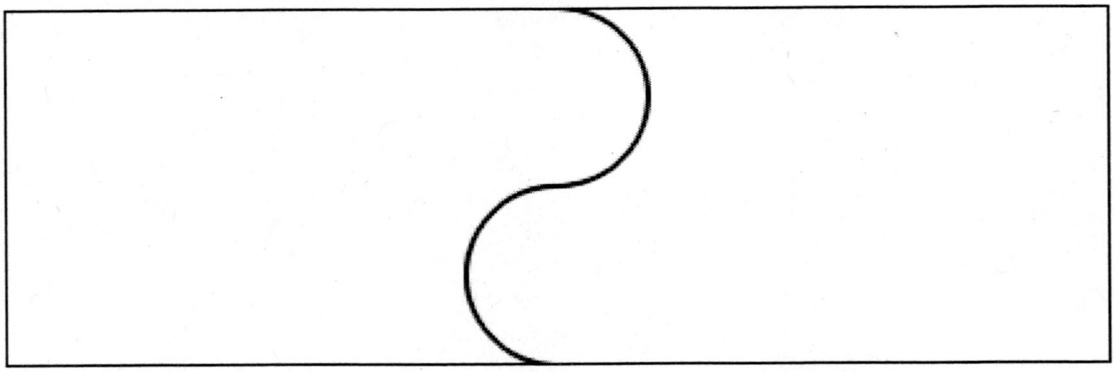

Dear Parents and Guardians,

We will be beginning a homework program designed to enrich your child's reading and writing development. Home support is indispensable in reinforcing and building upon emerging reading and writing skills. A Read and Write book will be sent home. In it you will find an envelope containing some small word cards.

The homework requires the following steps:

- Children arrange the word cards in as many different sentences as they can on a tabletop or work area.
- The parent's job is to print the sentence the child has chosen into the homework book for the child. The adult's neat printing provides the child with a reading selection to practice.
- The child then copies that sentence in his/her own printing and then illustrates the sentence.

The Read and Write books will come back to school each day and will become a part of your child's reading selections.

Thank you for your support,

Sincerely,

Read and Write books will be sent home on the following circled days

Mondays, Tuesdays, Wednesdays, Thursdays, Fridays

- Please return them the next morning so we may use them in class.

Dear Parents and Guardians,

We will be beginning a homework program designed to enrich your child's reading and writing development. Home support is indispensable in reinforcing and building upon emerging reading and writing skills. A Read and Write book will be sent home. In it you will find an envelope containing some small vocabulary word cards.

The homework requires the following steps:

- Students need to tell you about the word to ensure understanding.
- The students then write [ ] sentences using these words.
- The parent's job is to ask questions about the vocabulary and the sentences
- Discuss what is being read to

The Read and Write books will come back to school each day and will become a part of your child's reading selections.

Thank you for your support,

Sincerely,

Read and Write books will be sent home on the following (circled) days

Mondays, Tuesdays, Wednesdays, Thursdays, Fridays

- Please return them the next morning so we may use them in class.

About the Author

Teaching since 1986 in British Columbia, Canada, I have taught primary and intermediate grade levels, ESL and special needs classes. Experience with learning disabilities and behaviour issues in children have been an important part of my learning.

My own daughters, Jennifer and Jessica, taught me how important it is to instil success and confidence early in a child's experience with reading and writing. To build upon experiences children can relate to, to provide positive interactions, to learn by having fun are important elements that I believe need to be incorporated into effective teaching. Early on in my career I began developing my own teaching materials and have shared many techniques with colleagues.

Currently I am working on multiple publishing projects. Through the encouragement from colleagues, many parents and my family I decided to publish some teaching methods that had reached so many children.

I hope this is as effective for you as it has been for my students. Remember that while we are teachers, we are also the makers of memories, may they all be good ones.

Enjoy every moment with your children.

Lisa Peterson

"Nothing done for children is ever wasted."

~ *Mark Twain*

For further information on resources and upcoming publications and publishers' displays or for workshop presentation bookings please visit www.peterson-jensica.com

Making Sentences Theory and Research

FIVE PRINCIPLES

These 5 principles of effective pedagogy as set out by Christopher Wimer and Ronald F. Ferguson at Harvard University may seem familiar and even obvious.

1: Scaffold learning on students' prior knowledge
2: Present organizing schemas and frameworks
3: Help make key connections—don't assume they'll discover them.
4: Apply concepts in multiple ways and varied contexts
5: Teach children how to learn

Making Sentences encompasses all these elements. It is a hands-on, multilevel developmentally appropriate method of enhancing reading and writing in beginning students. Reading and writing go together. Writing supports reading and reading supports writing (Toronto District School Board). This program is based on over 20 years of classroom experience and the wisdom of many other professionals and researchers. Making Sentences has a sound basis in accessing prior knowledge, scaffolded instruction and brain research in order to make connections in reading and writing. Making Sentences is supported by oral language, visuals, cooperative games and activities.

It is important that reading components be taught within an integrated context (Lyon). Brain research suggests that the more ways we can provide for the students to experience concepts, through seeing, hearing, and manipulating, the more ways information is represented in the brain (Wolfe). Teaching concepts and providing varied and hands on practice activities contributes to the memory retention and recall (Wolfe).

Learning that can be connected to prior personal experience is more likely to be retained and more likely to be applied and connected to future learning. (Wunderlich, Bell, Ford). It is effective to plan our curricula, methods, and assessments according to the largest number of students, leaving few, if any, who need individualized accommodations (Wunderlich, Bell, Ford). Using experiences from the students' reality allows the teacher to open the doors to their world. Using their experiences as topics for reading and writing is powerful. These interactive aspects of reading and writing and oral language are vital to skill development (Depree & Iversen).

Scaffolding Instruction provides assistance until the child can do it alone. Making Sentences allows reluctant writers the ease of manipulating the word cards rather than pencil work. According to the McCrackens,' children need four things in order to write. Students need ideas, words, and structure and need to know how to spell. In addition to meeting these four guidelines, Making Sentences also provides for invented spelling. Children need to gain confidence in their ability to write (Goodman).

Writing frames can help beginning writers learn to write quickly and acquire writing skills and strategies (McCracken & McCracken). The use of frame sentences allows teachers to focus on sentence patterns and language conventions. Beginning readers should not be given too many sight words to memorize out of context (Goodman). Presenting familiar vocabulary in a methodical manner and providing varied reinforcement is helpful in establishing a learning centered environment.

According to our Provincial Quick Scale writing standards, the grade one rubric states that writing should be readable and make sense. A grade one student is able to write independently with occasional help, with writing displaying the following:

Meaning	- sentences or ideas are related
	- some detail
Style	- repeats simple patterns
	- some simple description
Form	- follows form modeled by teacher
	- writing can stand alone
Conventions	- upper and lower case
	- invented spelling
	- some punctuation

Making Sentences assists students in meeting criteria provided on the Writing Standards Rubrics. Students are supported while being taught to write sentences with appropriate use of upper and lower case, invented spelling, and some punctuation. Student writing will also display related ideas with the use of repeated simple patterns. Students are able to follow form demonstrated by the teacher.

I trust you will enjoy using Making Sentences with your beginning and/or ESL students. A great deal of thought and time has gone into its' creation. Every attempt has been made to select activities and to create a flow to the program to make it effective for you and your students.

References

Achieve BC Education. 2005. *Quick Scale Writing Standards.* Ministry of Education, Province of British Columbia

Baskwill, 1990. *J. New Directions. Connections a child's natural learning tool.* Newkirk Road, Richmond Hill, Ontario, Canada. Scholastic-TAB publications Ltd.

Cunningham, P.M. 1995. *Phonics They Use: Words for Reading and Writing. 2d ed.* New York: Harper Collins.

Cunningham, P.M. 1992.*What kinds of phonics instruction will we have?* In C.Kinzer & K. Leu (Eds.), Literacy research, theory, and practice: Views From man's perspectives. Chicago, IL: National Reading Conference, Inc.

Depree, H and Iversen, S. *Early Literacy in the Classroom.* 1994. Newkirk Road Richmond Hill, Ontario, Canada. by arrangement with Lands End Publishing New Zealand 11 Parliament Street, Lower Hutt

Fountas, I.C. and Pinnell, G.S.1998. *Word Matters.* Portsmouth, NH. Heinemann.

Peha, S. 2003.*There's No Practice Like Best Practice. Making Sense of the Research,* Recommendations and Rhetoric of Professional Teaching. <http://www.ttms.org/best_practice/best_practice.htm>11.24.06

Goodman, V. *Reading is More than Phonics.* 1995. Calgary Alberta Canada. Reading Wings.

National Council of Teachers of English. 2006. *NCTE Beliefs about the Teaching of Writing.* <http://www.ncte.org/about/over/positions/category/write/118876.htm> 11.24.06

National Institute of Child Health and Human Development National Institute if Health. 2006. *The NICHD Research Program in Reading Development, Reading Disorders and Reading Instruction.* <http://www.ncld.org/index.php?option=content&task=view&id=524>11.24.06

McCracken, Marlene J and McCracken, Robert A. 1979. *Reading, Writing, and Language.* Winnipeg, Canada. Penguis Publishers Limited

McCracken and Marlene J. McCracken. *Reading is Only the Tiger's Tail.* co 1972 Leswing Press San Rafael, California Robert A.,

Moline, S. *I See What You Mean. Children at Work with Visual Information.* Markham Ontario. Pembroke Publishers Limited

Pinnell, Gay S and Fountas, Irene C. *Word Matters.* 1998. Portsmouth, NH. Heineman. Toronto District School Board. Teaching Children to Read and Write. 2000.Toronto, Ontario

Wimer, C and Ferguson, R.F.2003. Brain Research and Learning *Implications for the Pedagogy Leg of the Tripod. Harvard University.* <http://www.ksg.harvard.edu/tripodproject/Brain%20Research%20&%20Implications%20for%20Tripod.pdf>11.24.06

Wolfe. Pat. PH.D Mind Matters Inc. *Brain Research and Education: Fad or Foundation?* < http://www.patwolfe.com/index.php?pid=100> 11.24.06

Wunderlich, K., Bell, A., Ford, *L.2005.* Learning Abstracts. Vol Jan. *Improving Learning Through Understanding of Brain Science Research.* http://www.league.org/publication/abstracts/learning/lelabs200501.html 11.24.06

Wylie, R.E. & Durrell, D.D. 1970. *Teaching Vowels Through Phonograms.* Elementary English, 47.

Lisa Peterson – Jensica Educational Support Services
Contact – www.peterson-jensica.com

MSMSMSMSMSMSMSMSMSMSMSMSMSMSMSMSMSMSMSMSMSMSMSMSMSMSMSMSMS

Lisa Peterson is available for professional development presentations as well as publishers displays. Be the first to learn new games and techniques that make learning fun and memorable.

Upcoming publications

Crazy Sentences – Sequel to Making Sentences
Fun Phrases – Grammar Games
Gotta Go – Math Resource for Rounding Off
Buddy Math – Math Resource for Regrouping
Vowel Sound Sort – Game

MSMSMSMSMSMSMSMSMSMSMSMSMSMSMSMSMSMSMSMSMSMSMSMSMSMSMSMSMS

Making Sentences

Jensica Educational Support Services

ORDER FORM FOR MAKING SENTENCES MATERIALS – CANADA

Number		Price	Total
	Making Sentences Manual	30.00	
	Mini Book package – to compliment manual	20.00	
	Picture cards – to compliment manual	15.00	
	Overhead cards – to compliment manual	5.00	
	Magnetic word cards – playground theme	5.00	
	Theme sequels for Making Sentences	25.00	
	Farm		
	Home		
	School		
	Community		
	Camping		
	Neighbourhood		
	Beach		
	Science Centre		
	Chuckles – cloze package of jokes for added fun	30.00	
	Making Sentences Package *Includes: manual, mini books, picture cards, and overhead cards.*	60.00	
	Shipping and Handling within BC $10.00 All orders outside BC tba		
	Tax included		
	TOTAL		

Orders may be emailed to Peterson@peterson-jensica.com
The Fax number and a mailing address are accessible at www.peterson-jensica.com

Name ______________________________ [please print]

Address ______________________________ Prov.________

Postal Code/Zip ________________ Email ______________________

School ______________________________ SD#____________

Telephone ________________________ Fax______________________

Signature ______________________________________

Lisa Peterson **Phone 604 908 9010**

Email: Peterson@peterson-jensica.com

www.peterson-jensica.com All prices subject to change - See website for current and US